The Artwork of 3ichael 7ambert
Volume IV

By

Michael Andrew Lambert Jr

Prologue

Welcome to "The Artwork of 3ichael 7ambert: Volume IV," a thoughtfully curated showcase of my artistic journey. This book serves as a glimpse into my creative universe, highlighting the variety of mediums and styles that have shaped my work throughout the years. From detailed drawings and vibrant paintings to groundbreaking multimedia creations, each piece conveys a story, captures a fleeting moment, or delves into a concept that holds personal significance for me.

My artistic inspiration stems from a mix of intuition, creativity, and a passion for problem-solving. Through my art, I strive to stir emotions, provoke thought, and forge a deeper connection with my audience. Whether you find yourself captivated by the intricate details of a sketch, the striking brushwork of a painting, or the layered complexity of a multimedia work, I hope each page encourages you to see the world from my perspective.

Thank you for taking the time to delve into this collection. I invite you to accompany me on this journey through the development of my artistic voice, and I sincerely hope my creations resonate with you as profoundly as they do with me.

Dedication

This book is a tribute to the amazing peers, teachers, and mentors who have influenced my artistic journey.

I want to express my gratitude to my Art Teachers at Rangeview High School, Kyle Riggins and Jennifer Minor. Your support and encouragement have allowed my creativity to flourish and have inspired me to delve into the depths of my imagination. The foundation you provided has been essential to my love for the arts.

To my mentor at Rocky Mountain College of Art and Design, your guidance and perspective have been crucial in my development as an artist. Your faith in my abilities has motivated me to challenge myself and keep growing.

Thank you all for being integral to my artistic journey. This collection embodies the knowledge, inspiration, and support you have shared with me.

Artist Statement

I am a multimedia artist who views art as more than mere creative expression; it's a lifestyle. To me, art goes beyond traditional boundaries, manifesting in every facet of life. Whether I'm painting, drawing, working with digital media, or sculpting, my creations reflect the belief that creativity knows no limits and is always present.

In my artistic journey, I experiment with a variety of materials and techniques, never limiting myself to a single form or style. Each artwork I produce is a testament to my conviction that art is omnipresent, just waiting to be uncovered and shaped. My process is both intuitive and experimental, allowing the journey to inform me as much as the initial idea.

For me, art transcends mere visual appeal; it's about living genuinely, appreciating the beauty in everyday experiences, and discovering inspiration in the unexpected. My creations invite others to view the world through this perspective, encouraging them to recognize the artistry in their own lives and to connect with the creativity that surrounds us.

Through my work, I strive to dissolve the lines between various mediums and disciplines, creating a rich tapestry of experiences, emotions, and concepts. My aim is not only to produce visually striking pieces but also to motivate others to embrace an artistic lifestyle, seeing the potential for art in all their endeavors.

In this sense, my art serves not just as a reflection of my creative vision but as a call to integrate art into the very fabric of life—a journey that encompasses both creation and discovery.

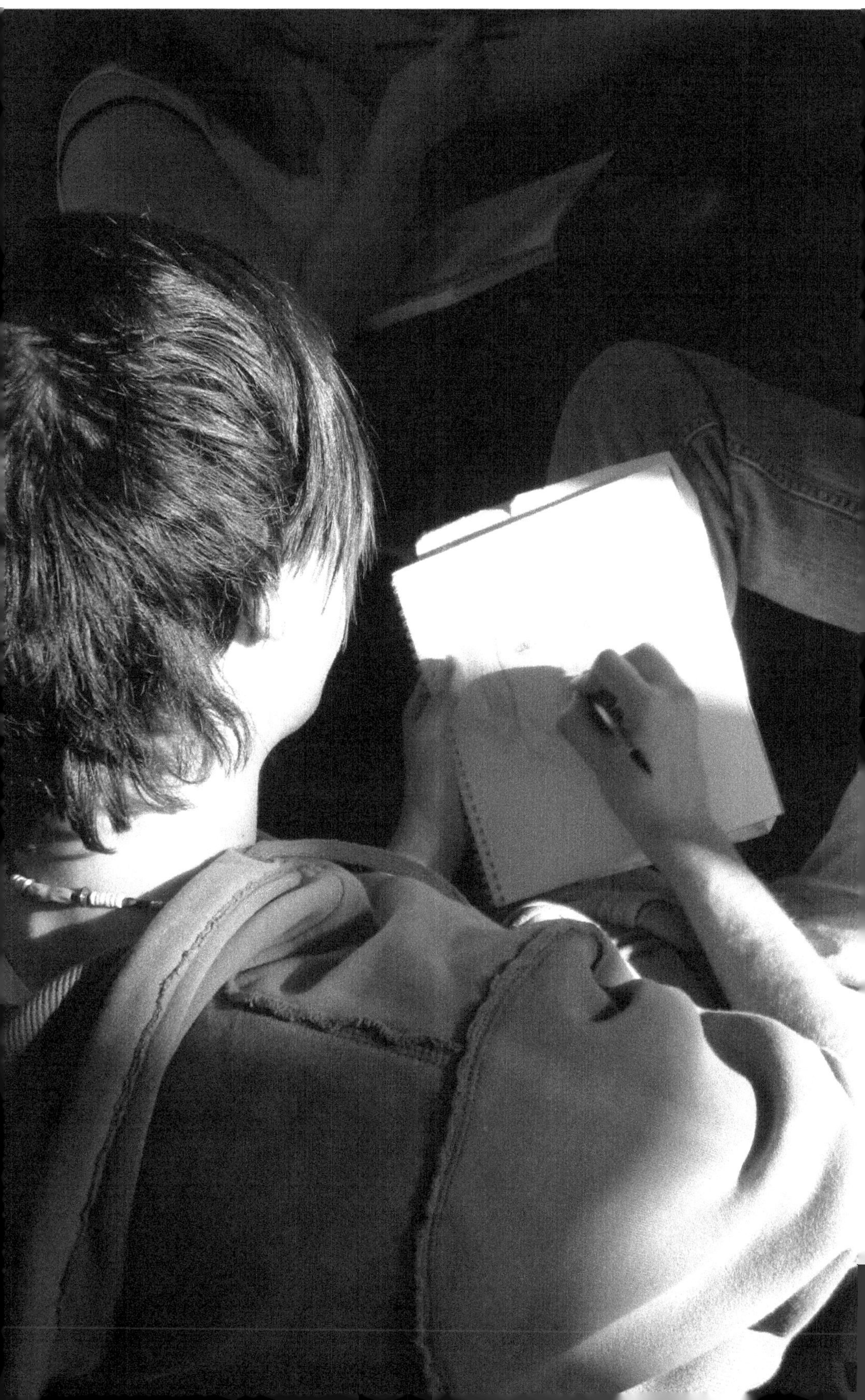

"PenPals Pencil"
2018
Digital Illustration

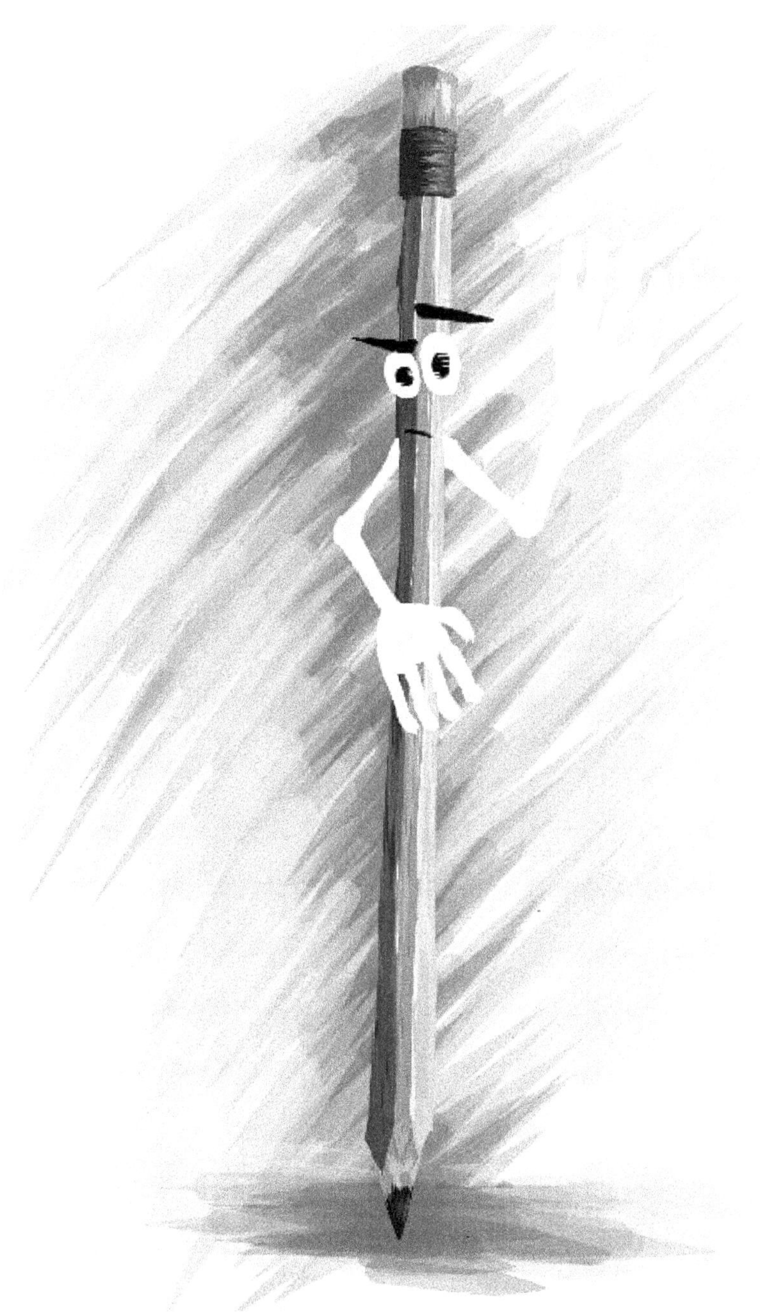

"Raiders and PenPals Promo"
2018
Digital

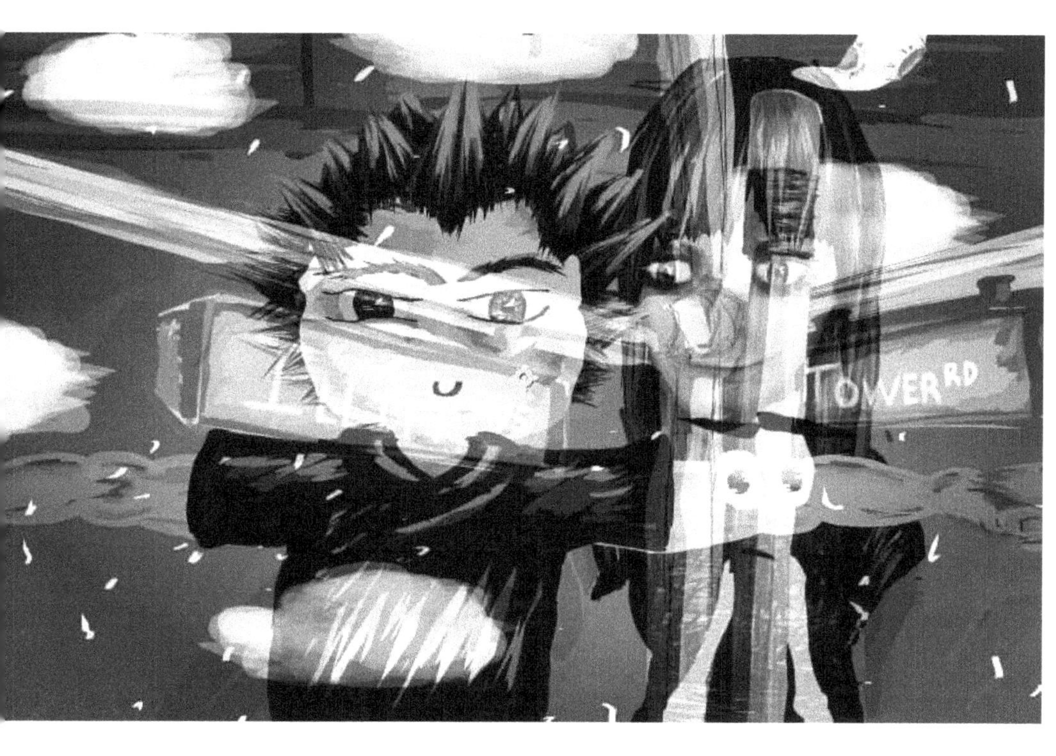
OWER RD

"The Paper Arcade Promo"
201
Game

"Color Pencil Asteroids Promo"
2016
Game

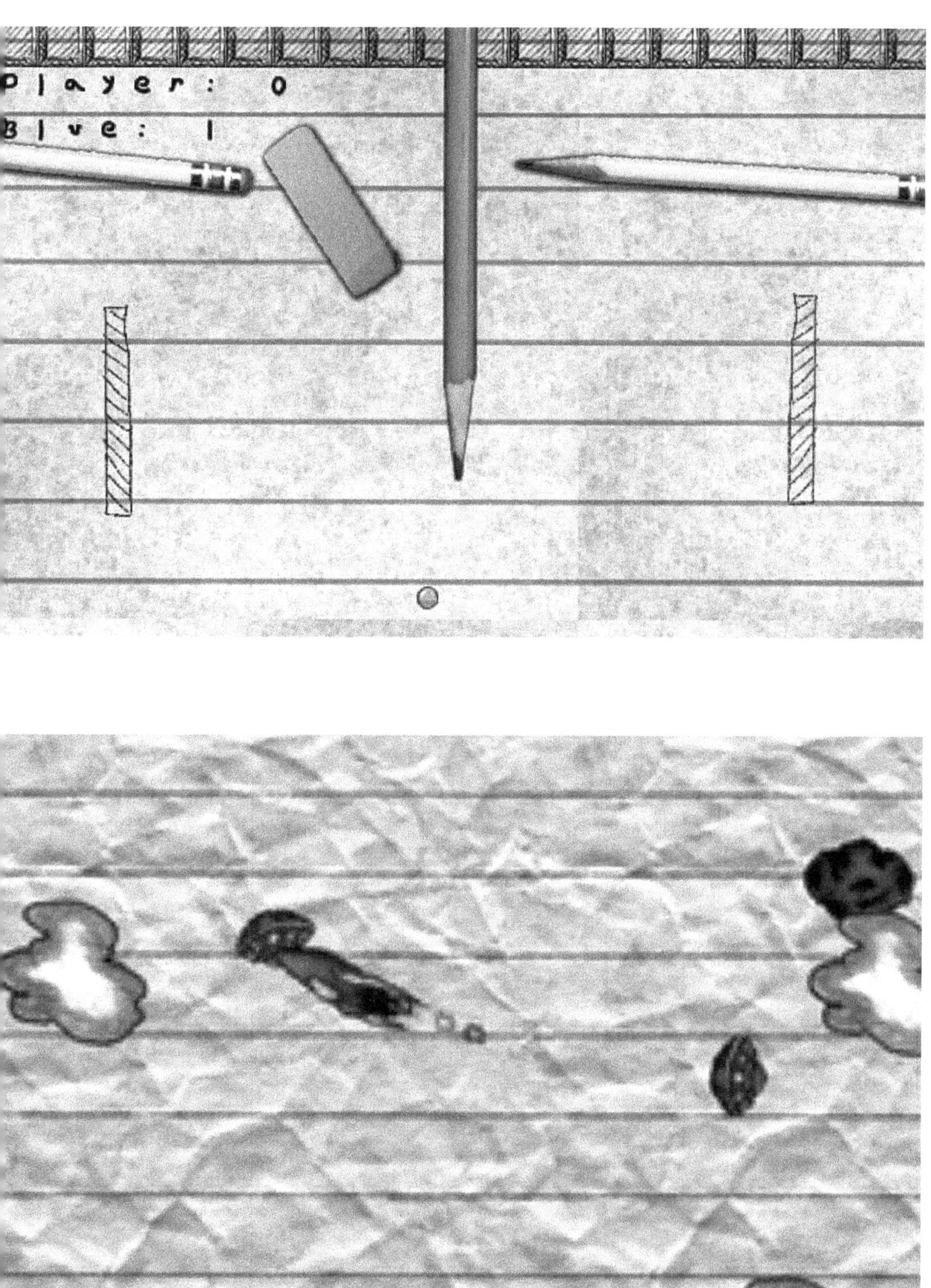
player: 0
Blve: 1

"Dillingham Owl"
2018
Digital

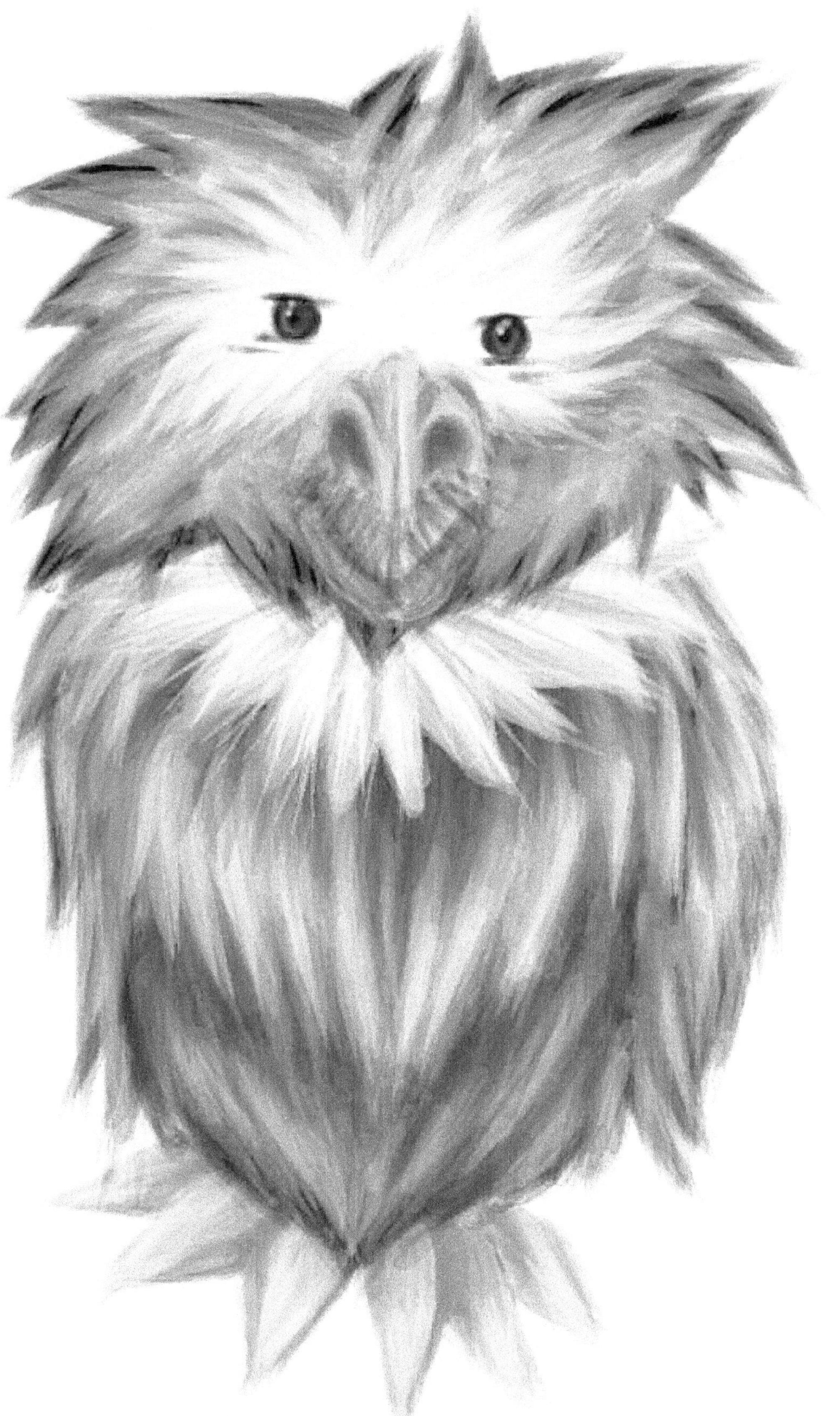

"SSJ5"
2005
Mechanical Pencil

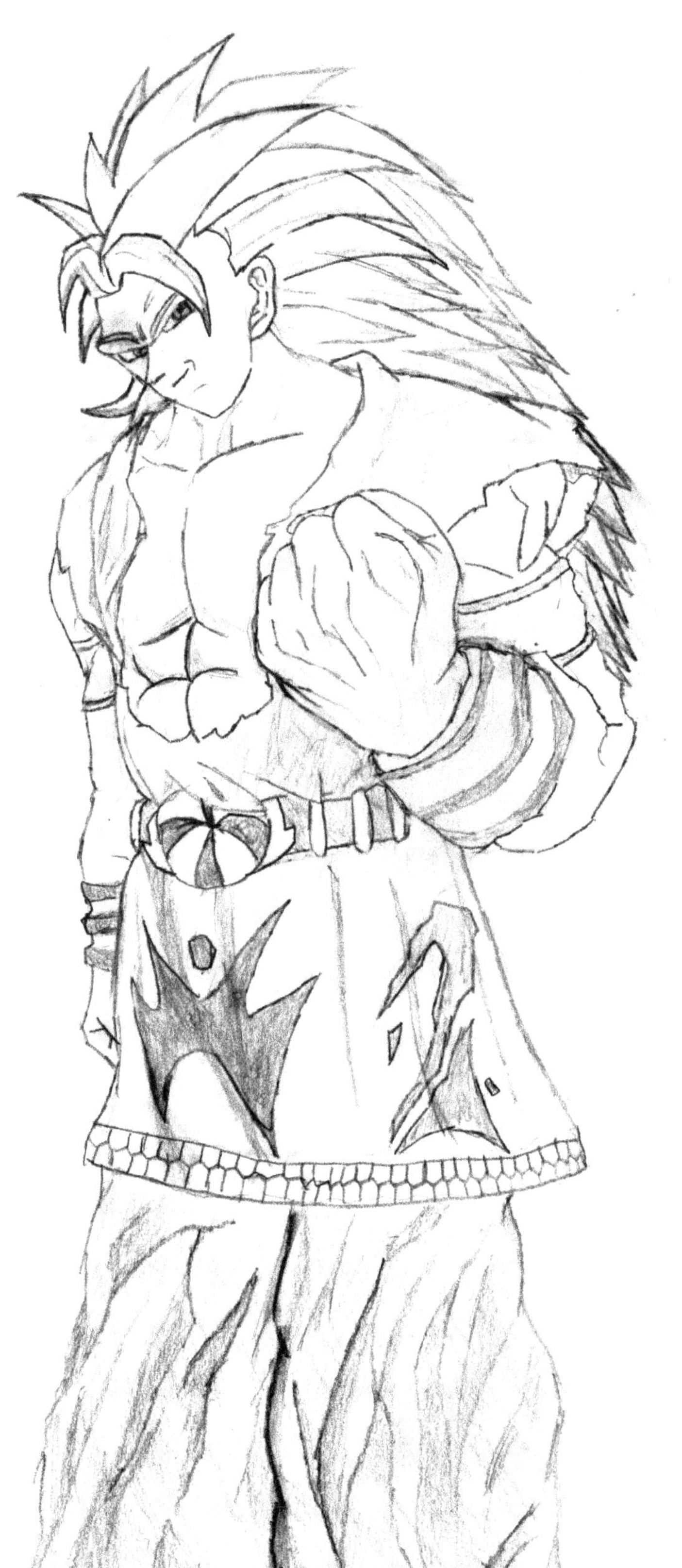

"Sketchbook Excerpt"
2008
Graphite and Ink

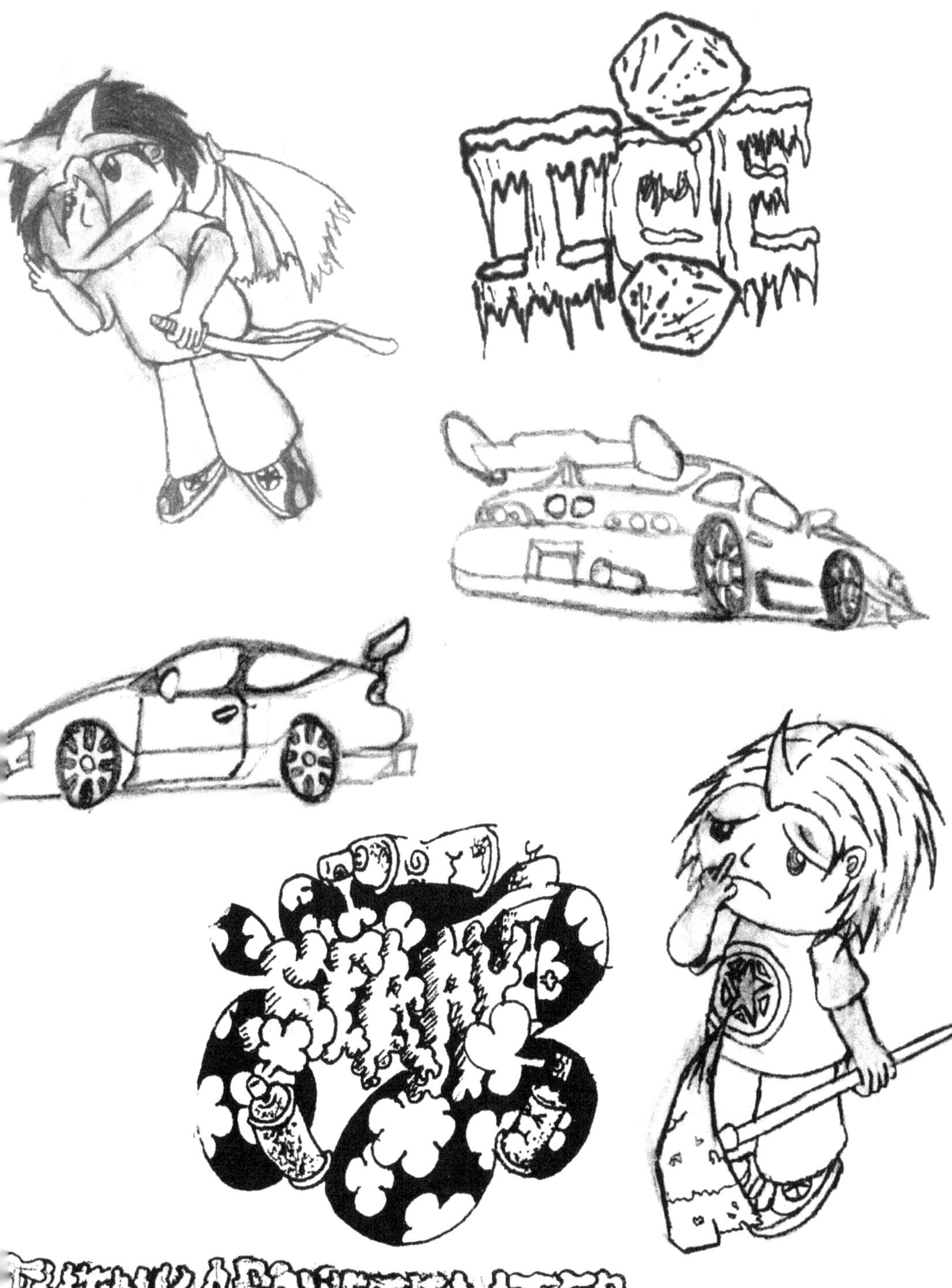
ICE
THINKABOUTITLATER

**"The Paper Arcade: PacMan
(screenshot)"**
2013
Game

"The Paper"
2016
Game

"Hope & Despair Cover #2"
2016
Game

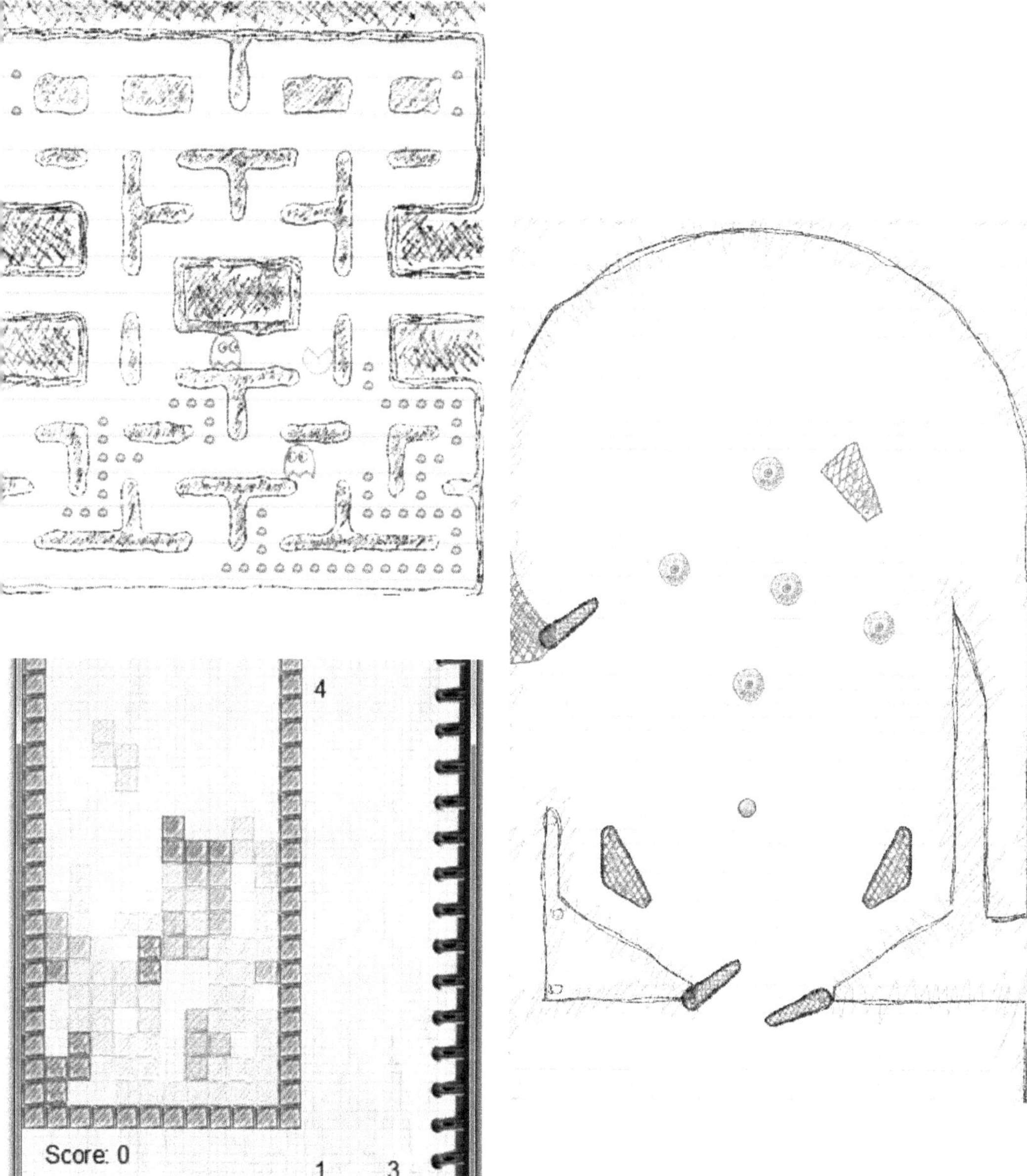
4
Score: 0
1   3

"Orpheus Unlimited Records"
2012
Website

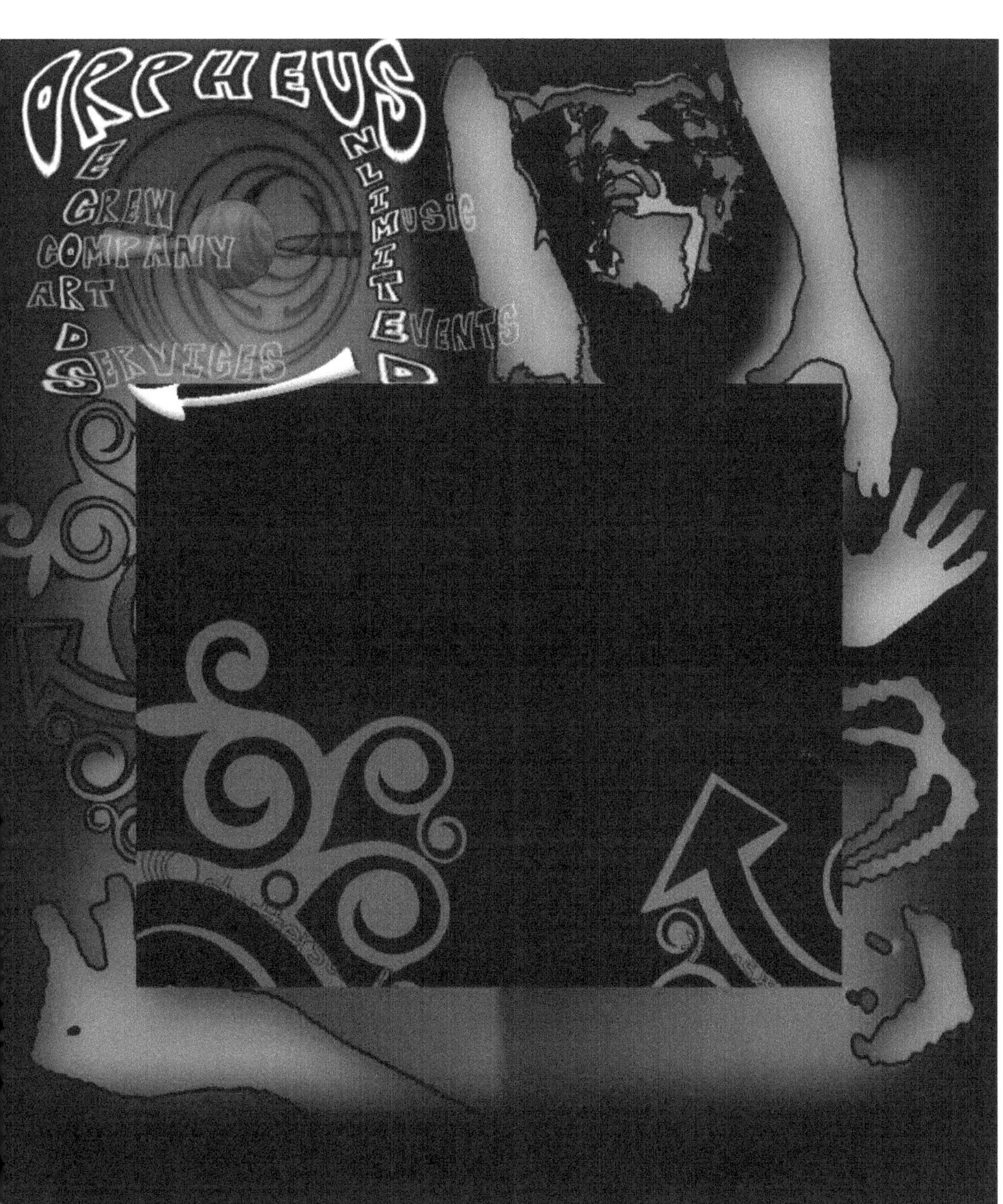
ORPHEUS
THE CREW COMPANY ART AND SERVICES
UNLIMITED MUSIC EVENTS UNLIMITED

"Sora"
2016
Digital

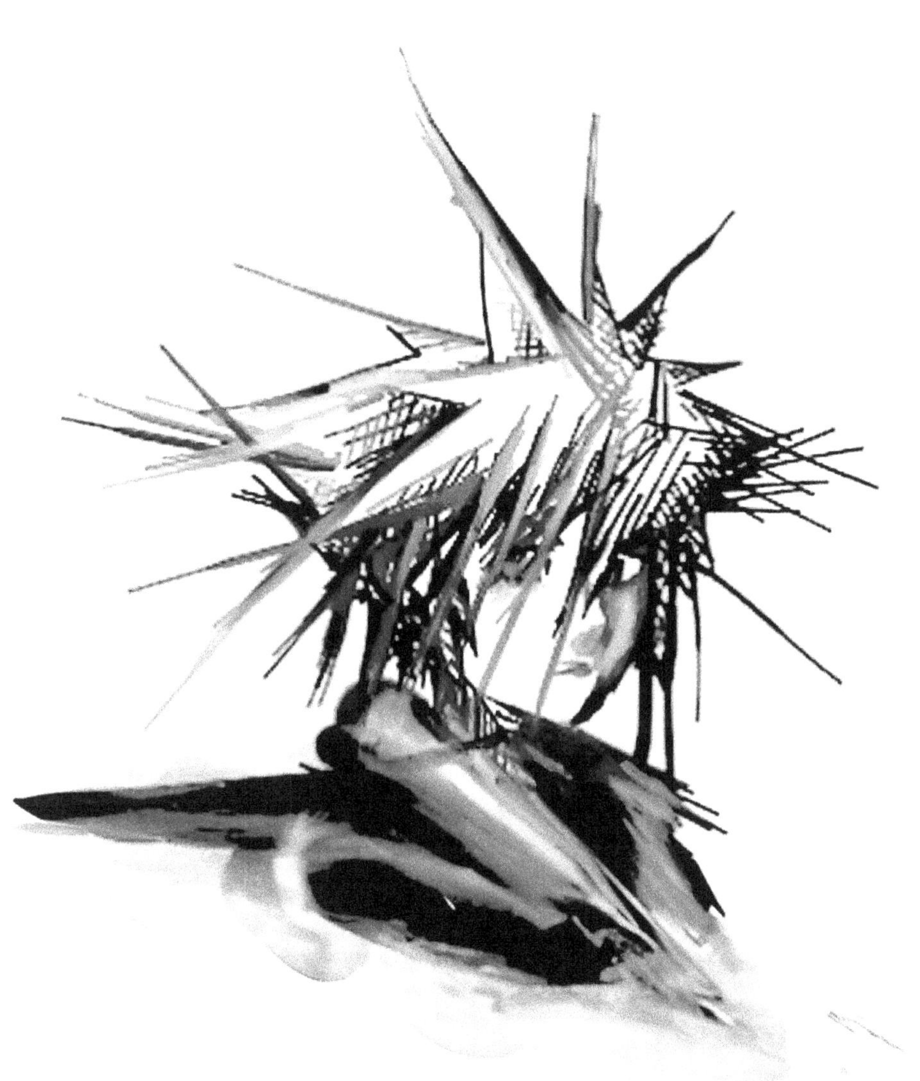

"Gumballs"
2016
Digital

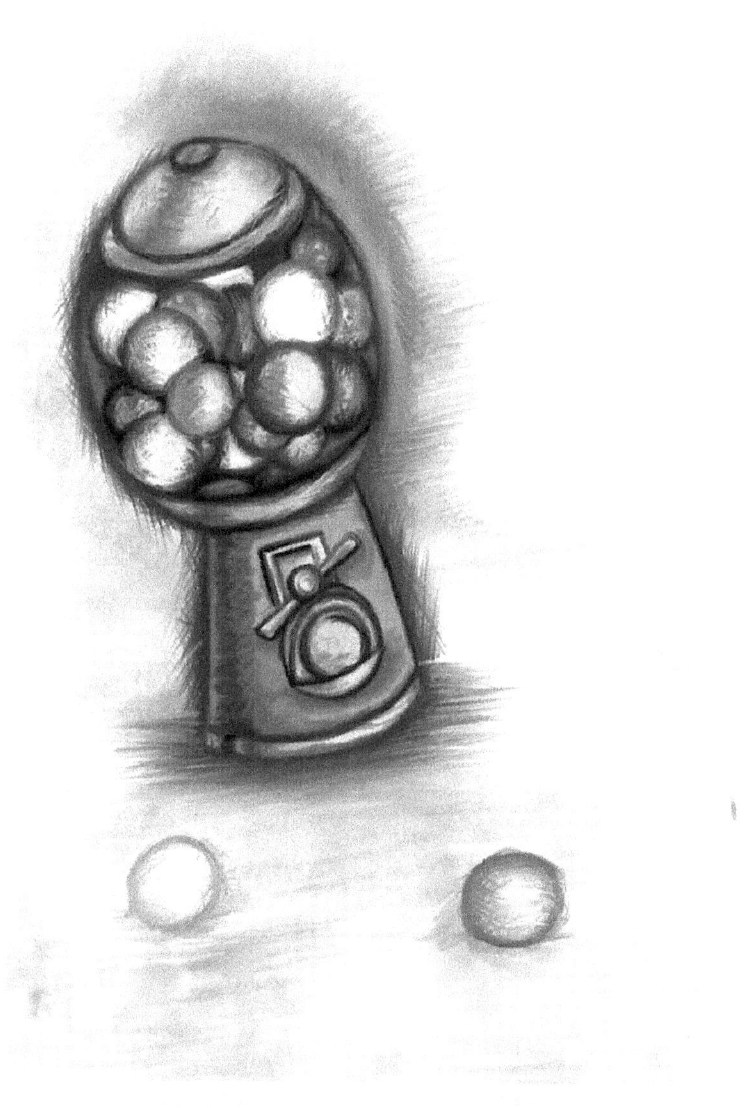

"Hope and Despair"
2018
Digital

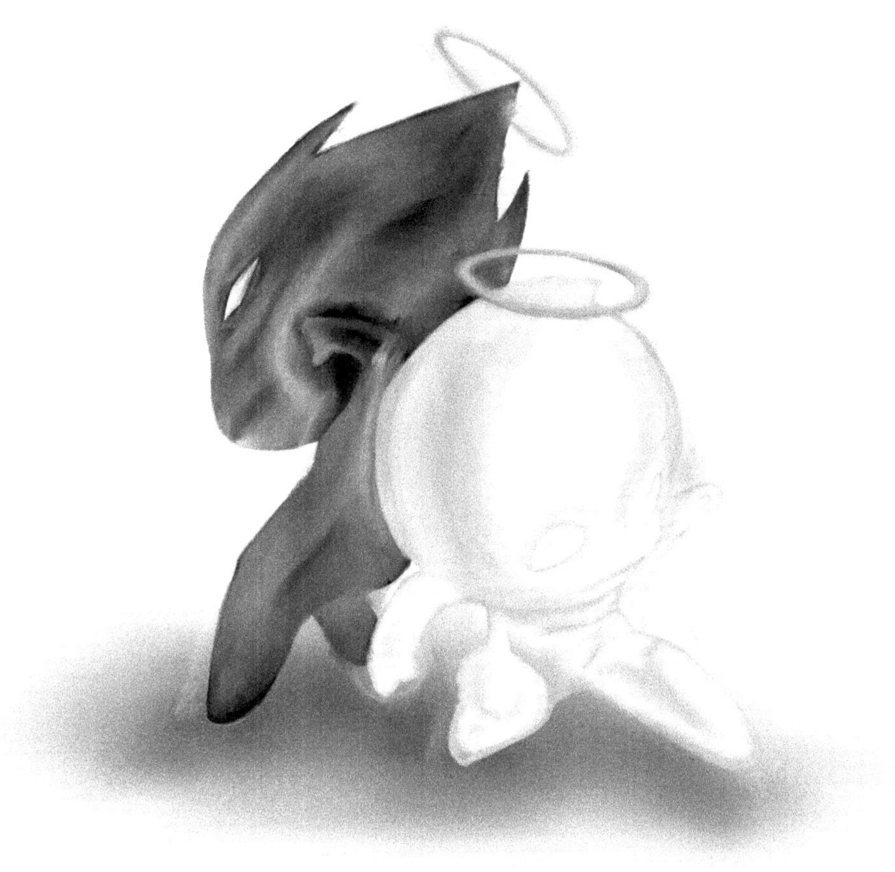

"Lady of the Lake"
2019
Digital

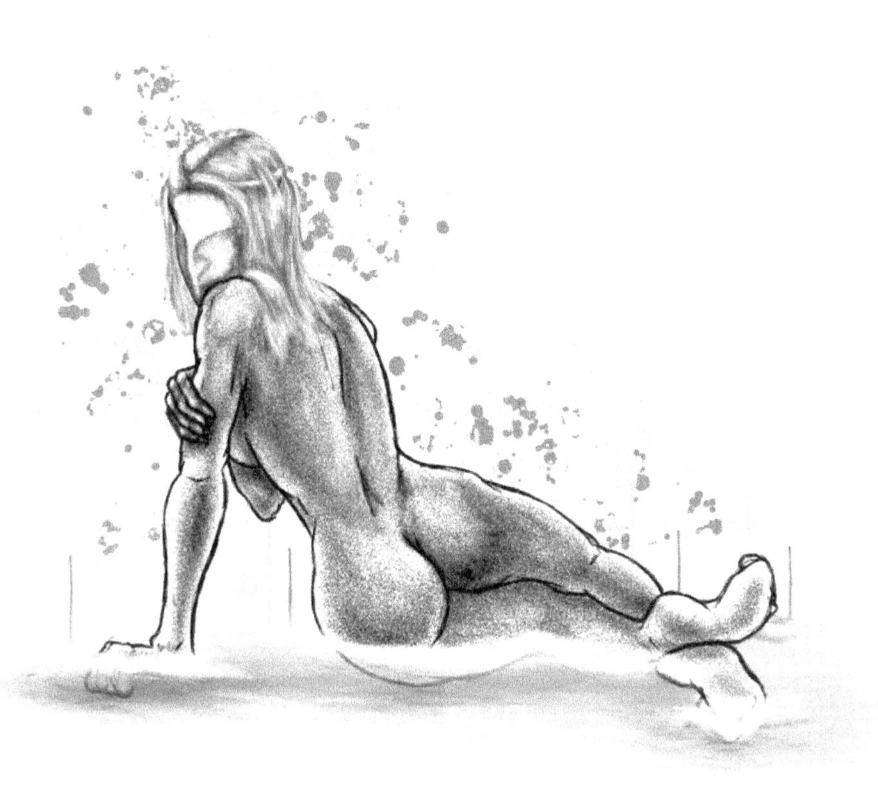

"Snowboard:: Odonis and Psy"
2019
Digital

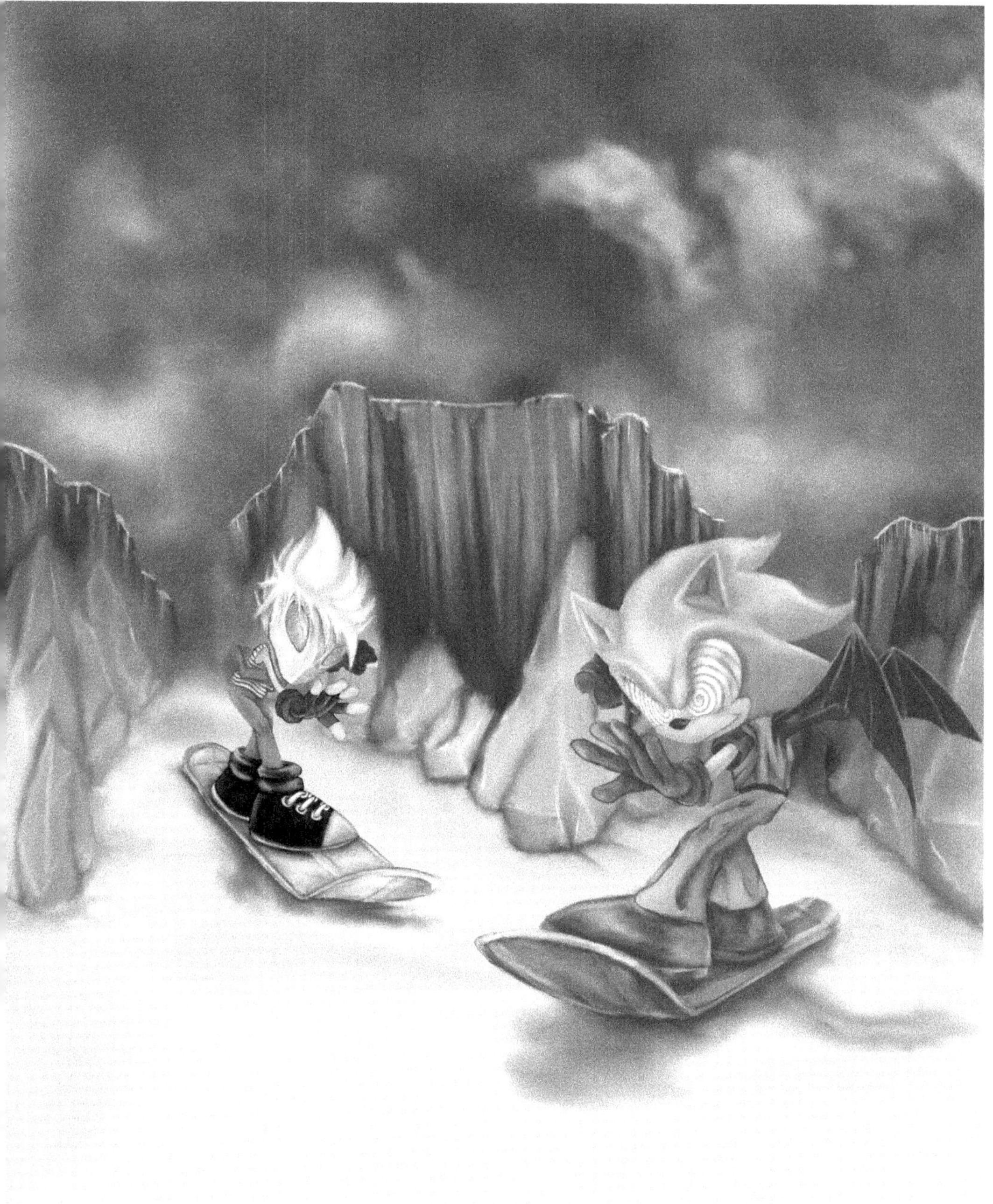

"Hope and Despair Humanoids"
2019
Digital

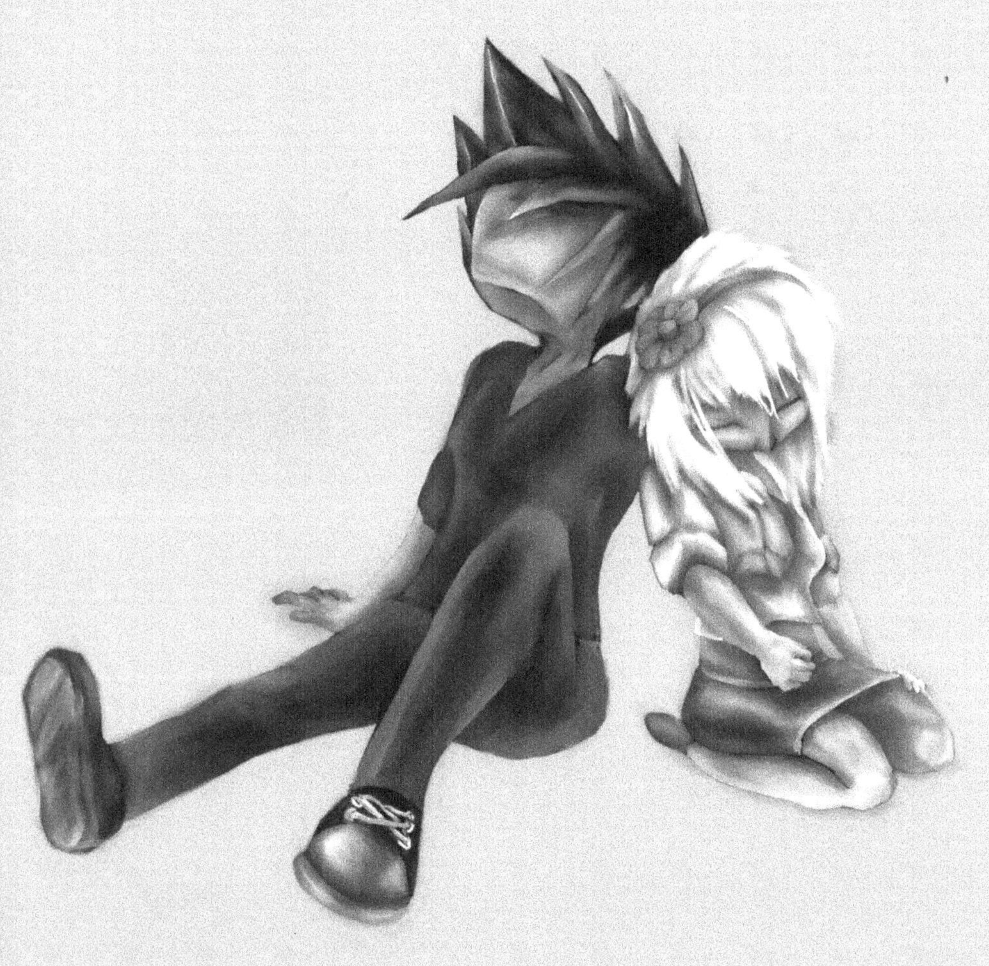

"Bee"
2018
Photography

"Fly"
2018
Photography

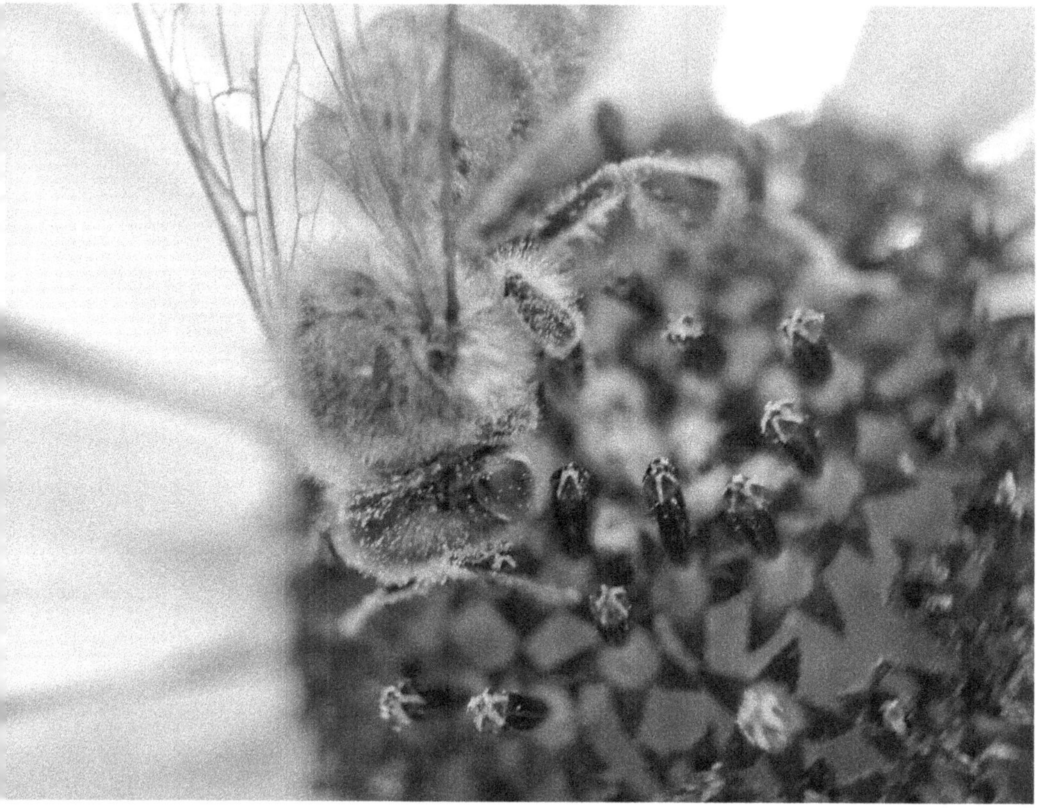

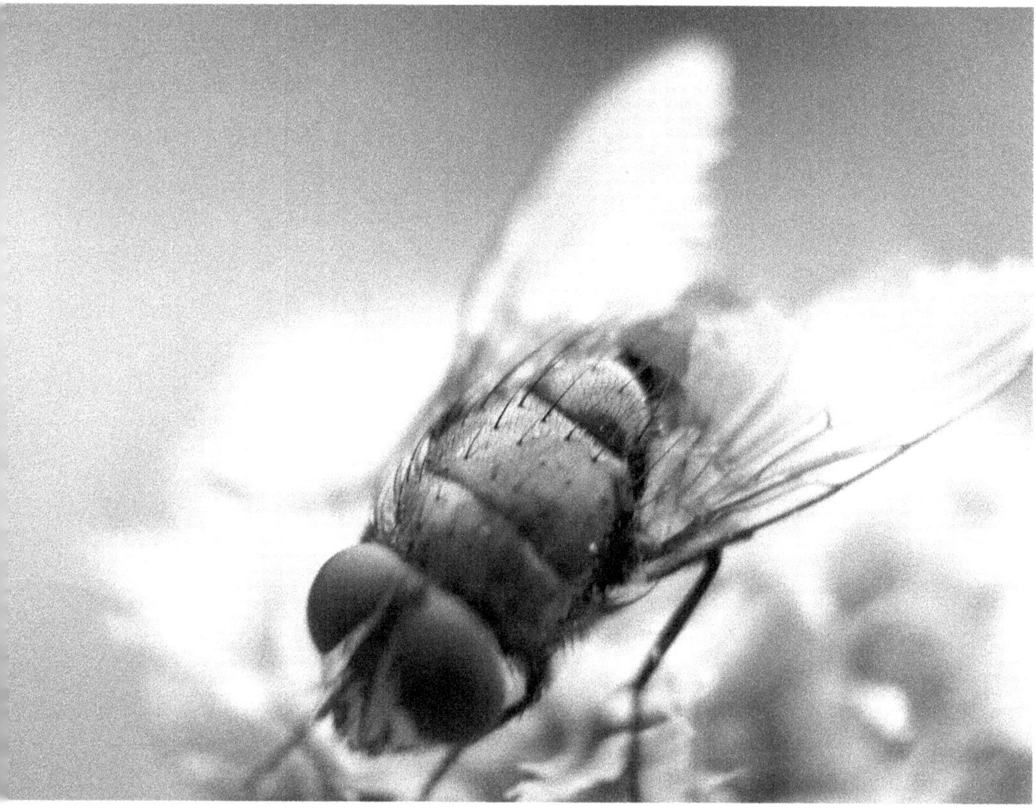

"Sneezeweed #1"
2018
Photography

"Sneezeweed #2"
2018
Photography

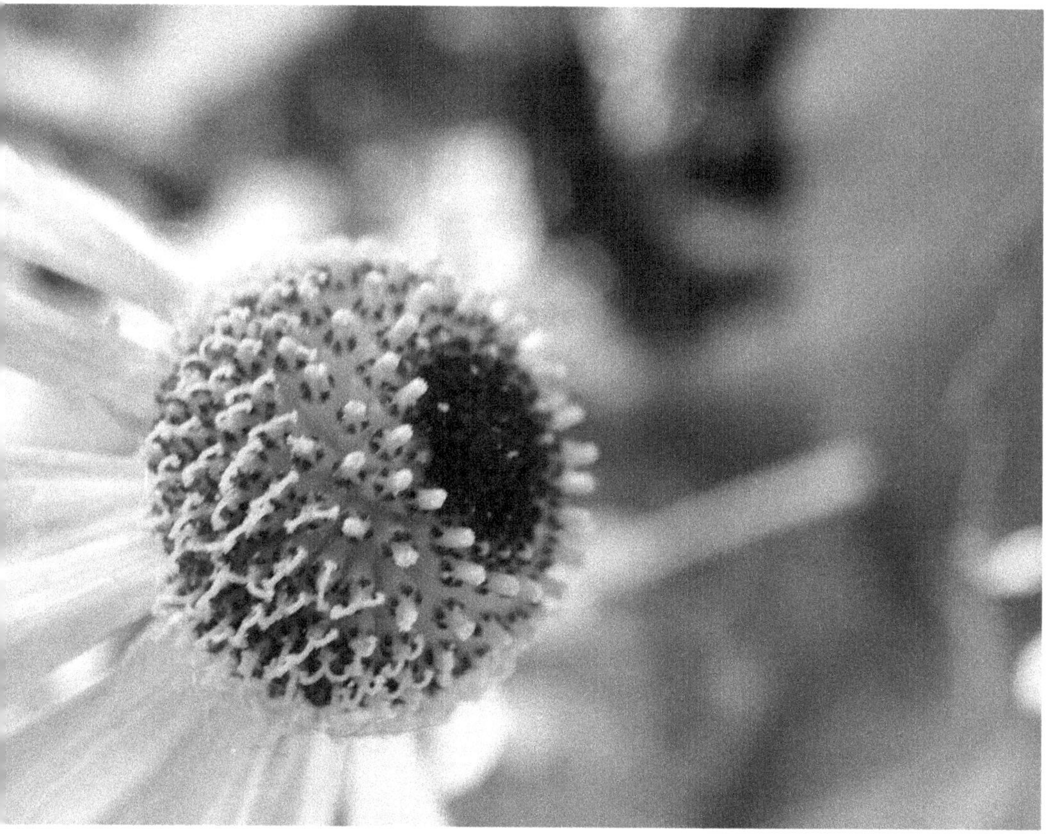

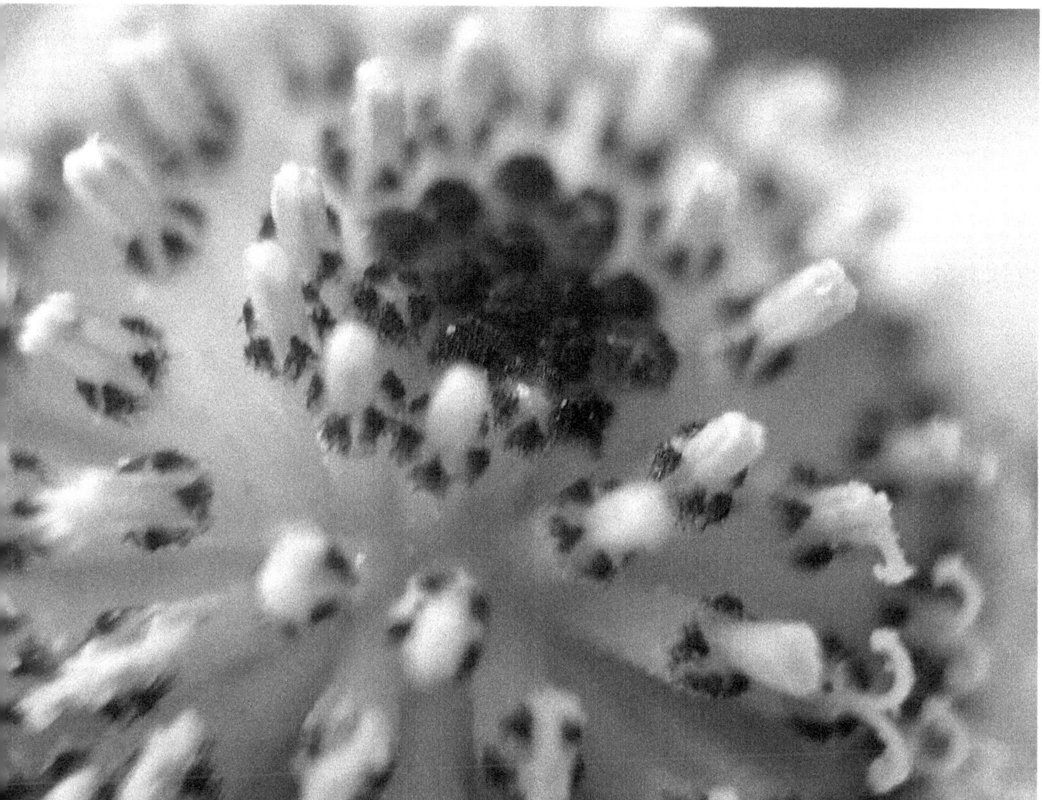

"Avalanca Promo"
2013
Game

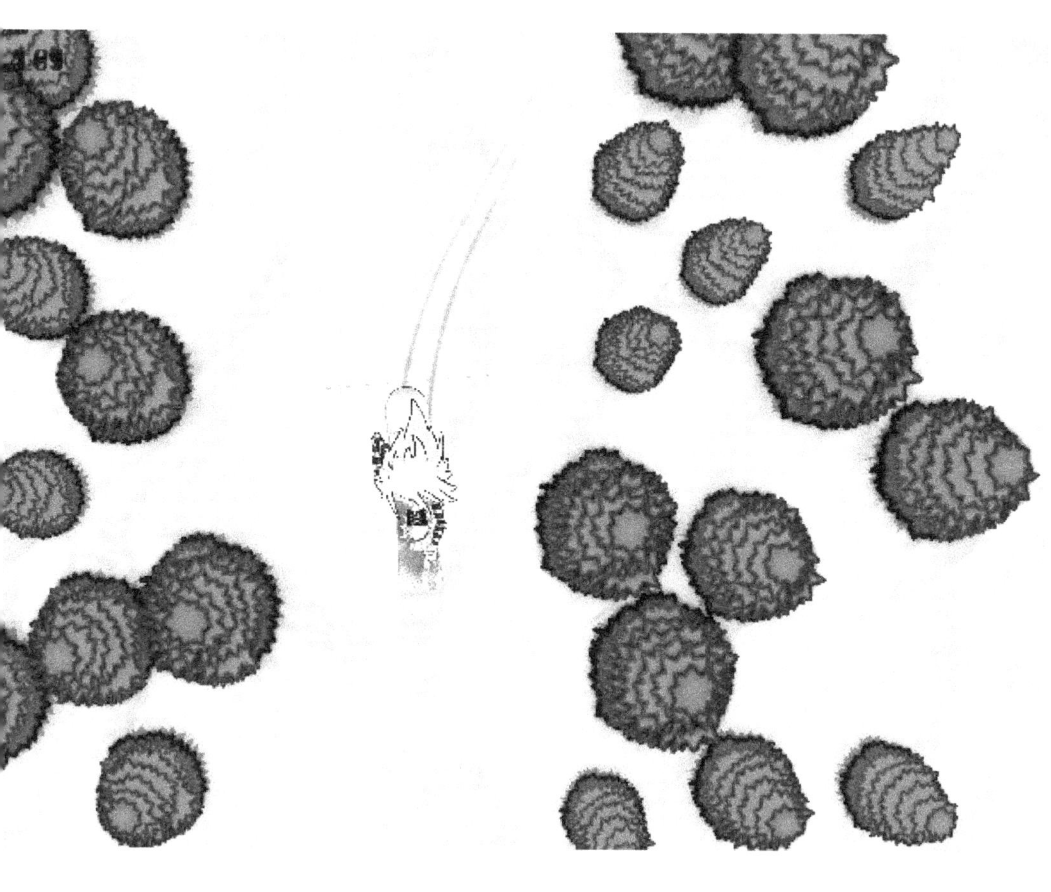

"Mobile Selfie"
2018
Photography

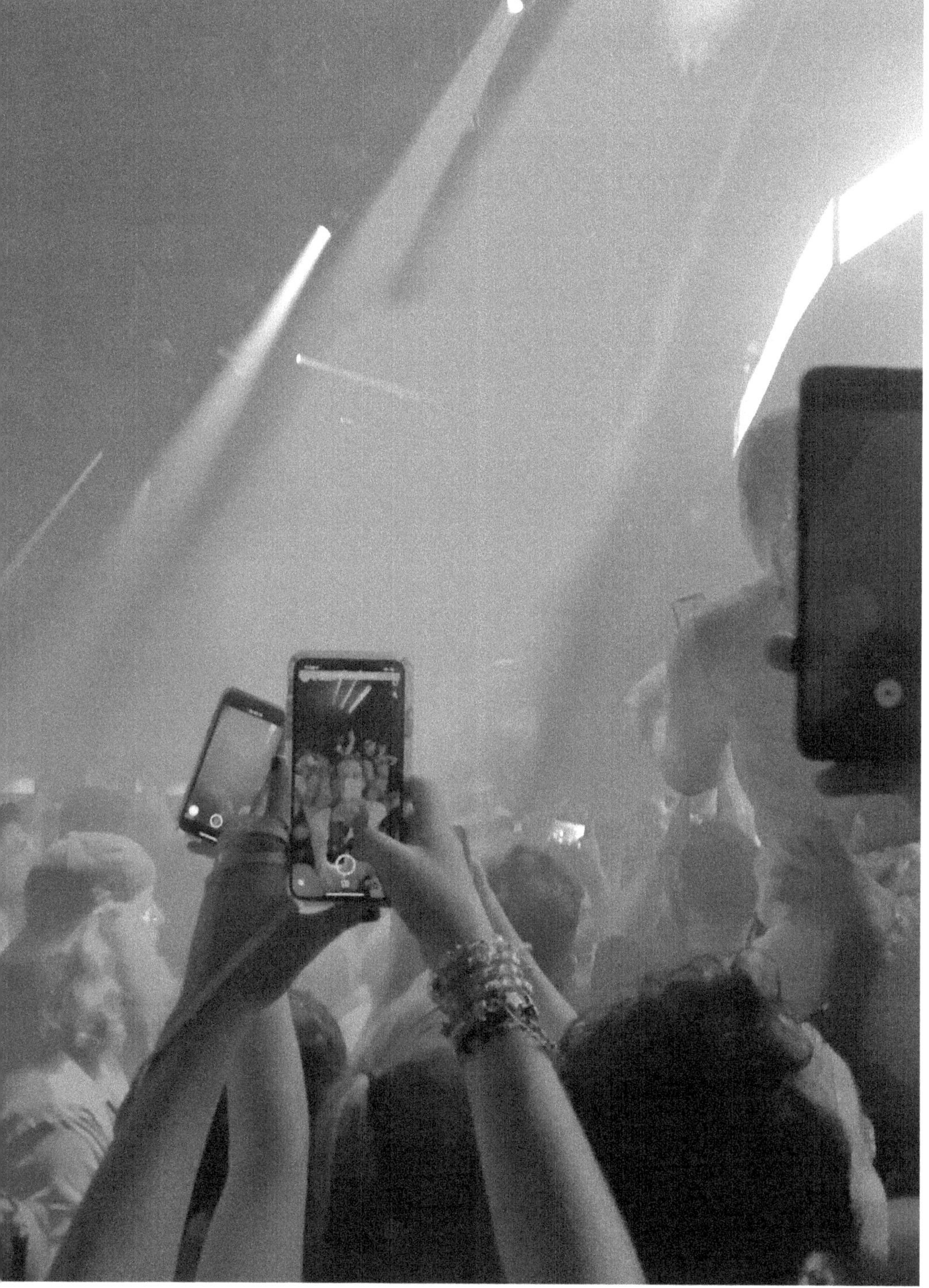

"Blue Girl"
2019
Digital

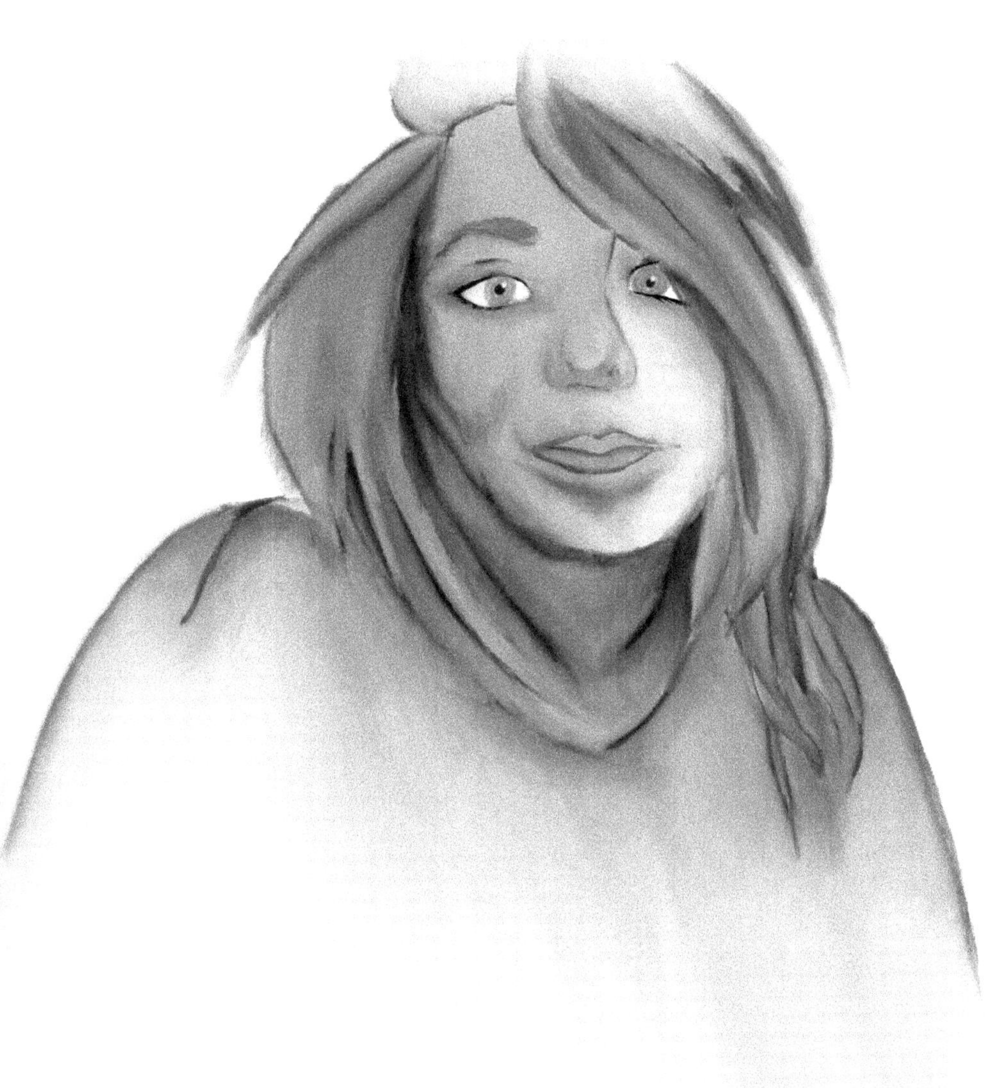

"He and Her"
2019
Digital

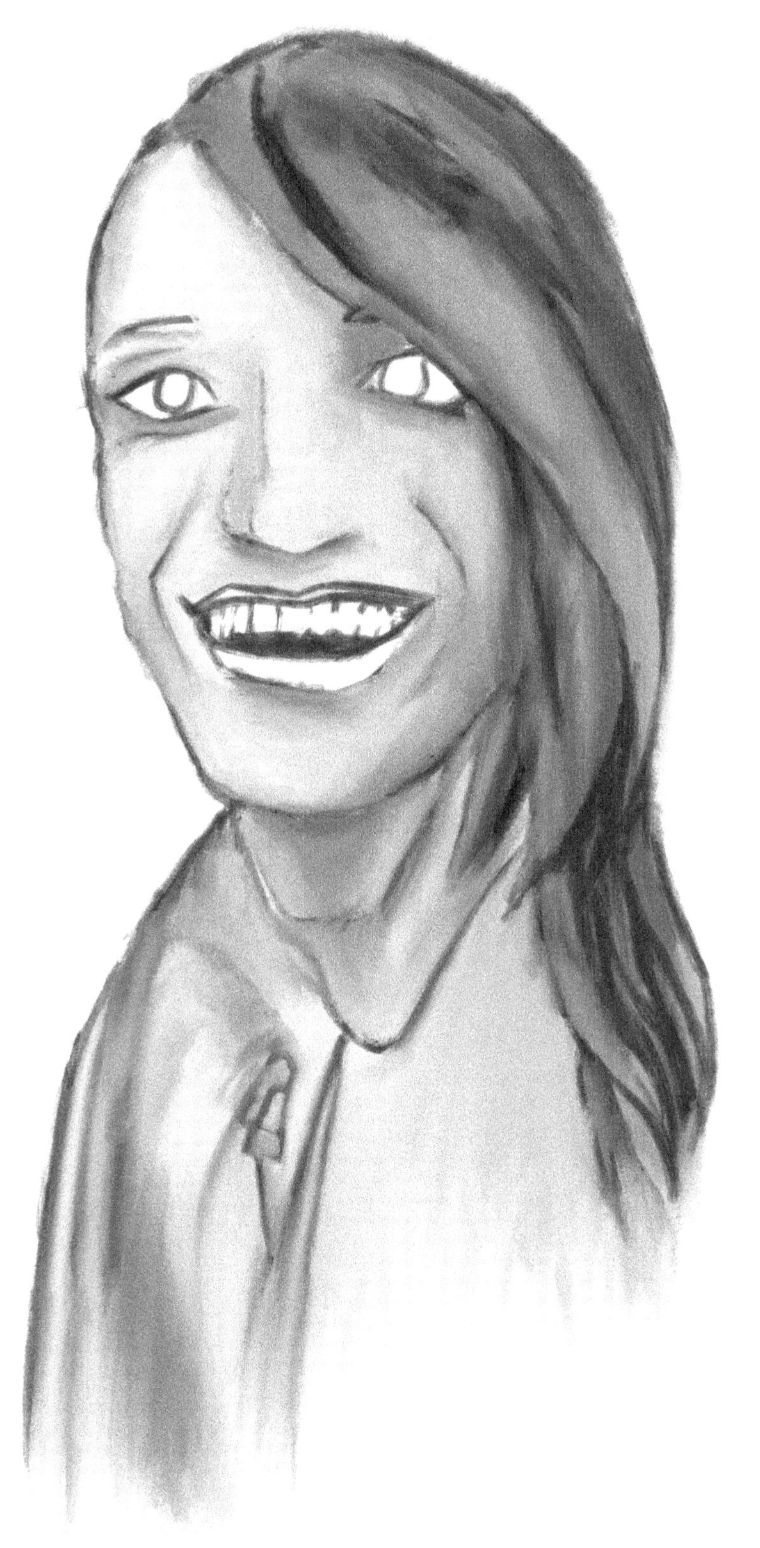

"Brown Girl Sketch"
2019
Digital

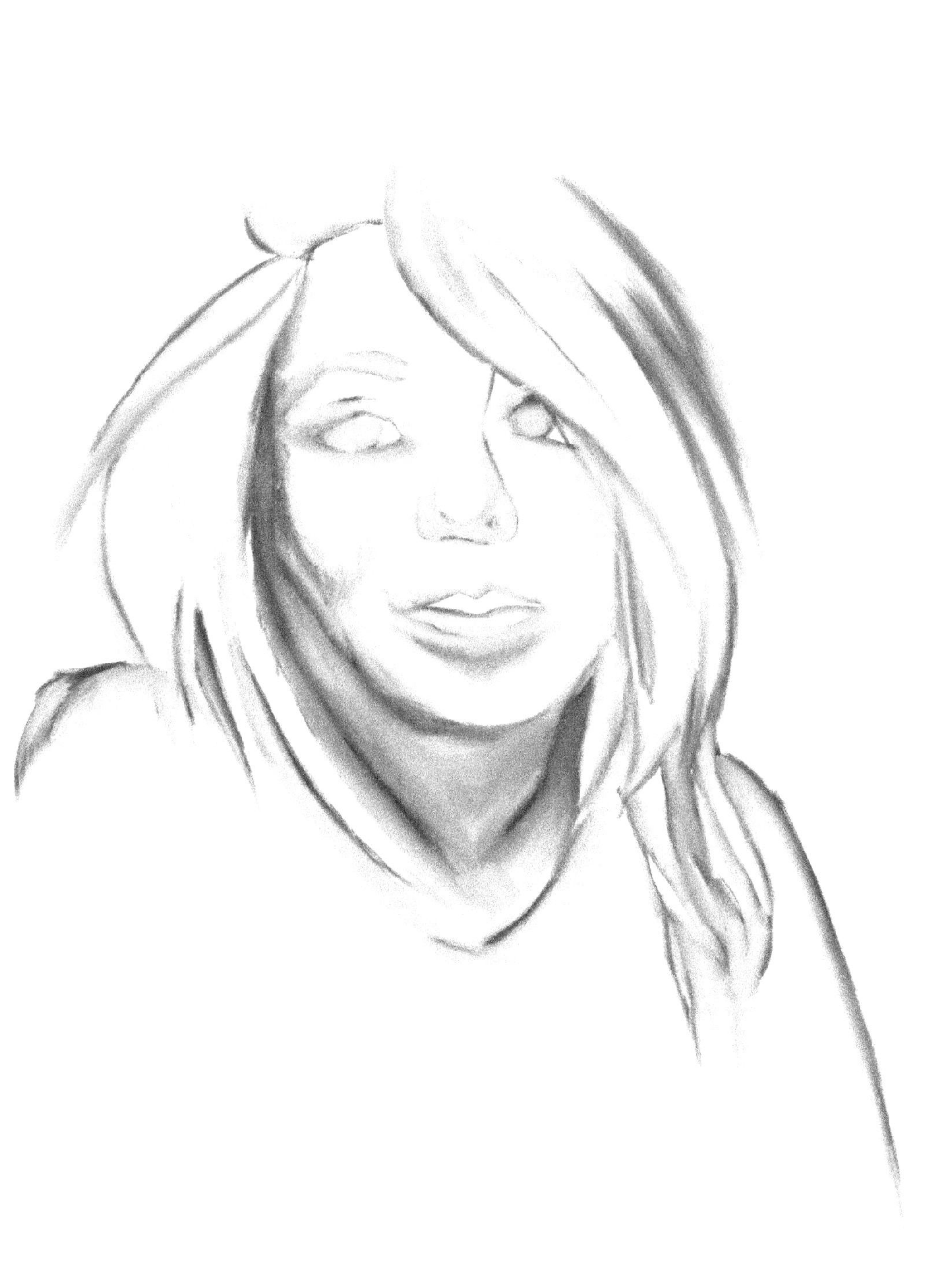

"Her Him Sketch"
2019
Digital

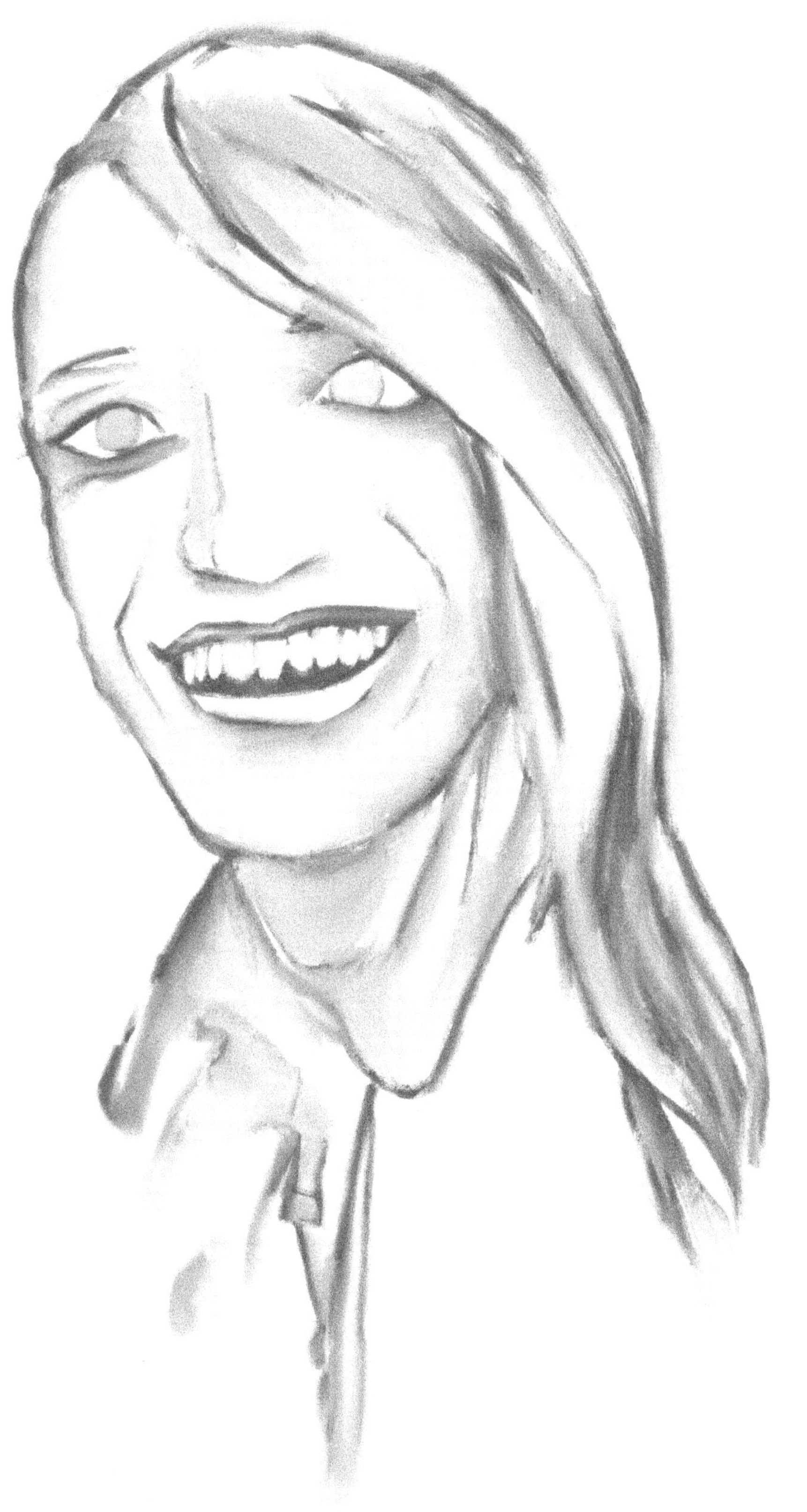

"Dillingham Little Planet"
2019
Digital

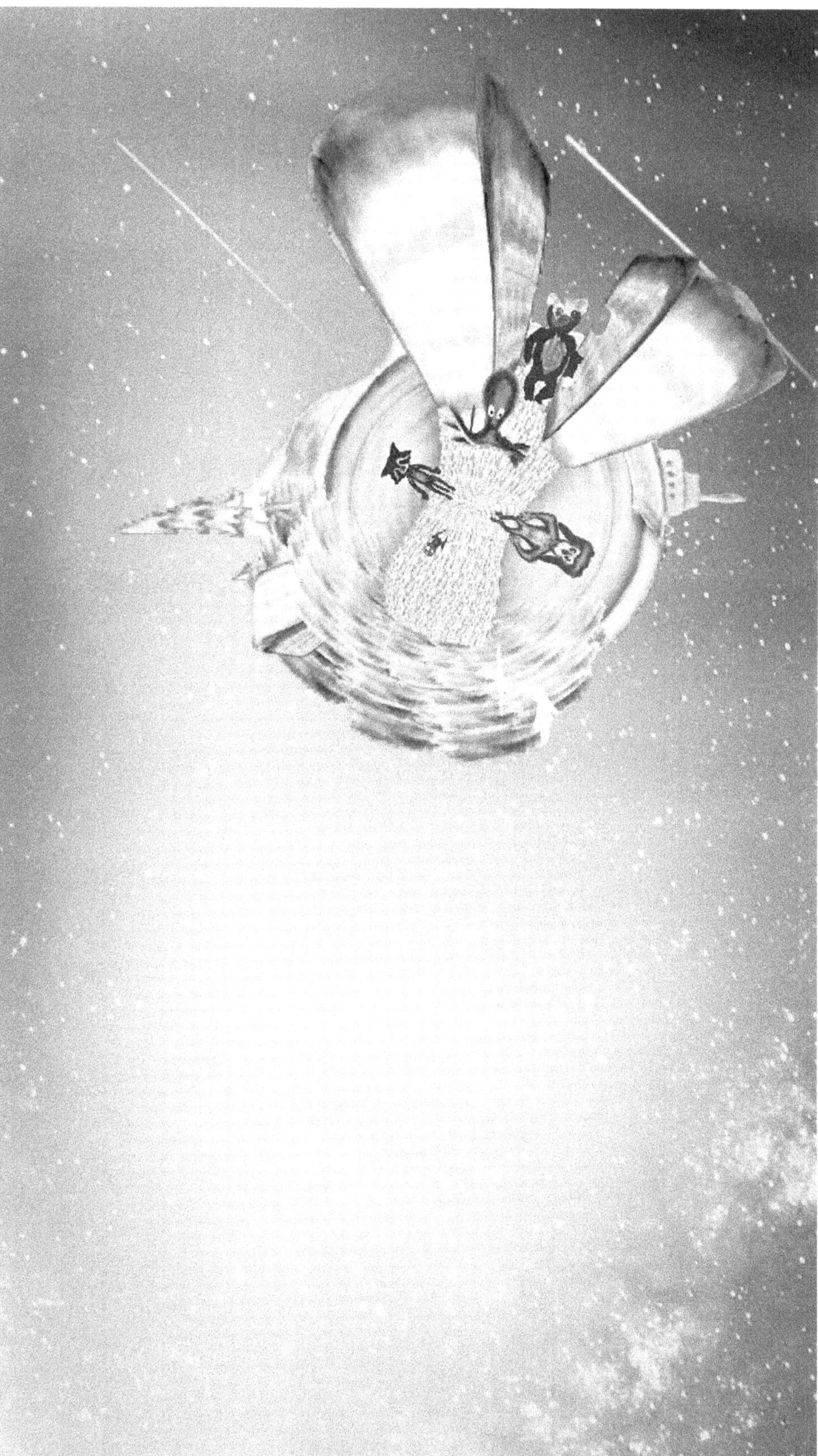

"Collision Course"
2018
Digital

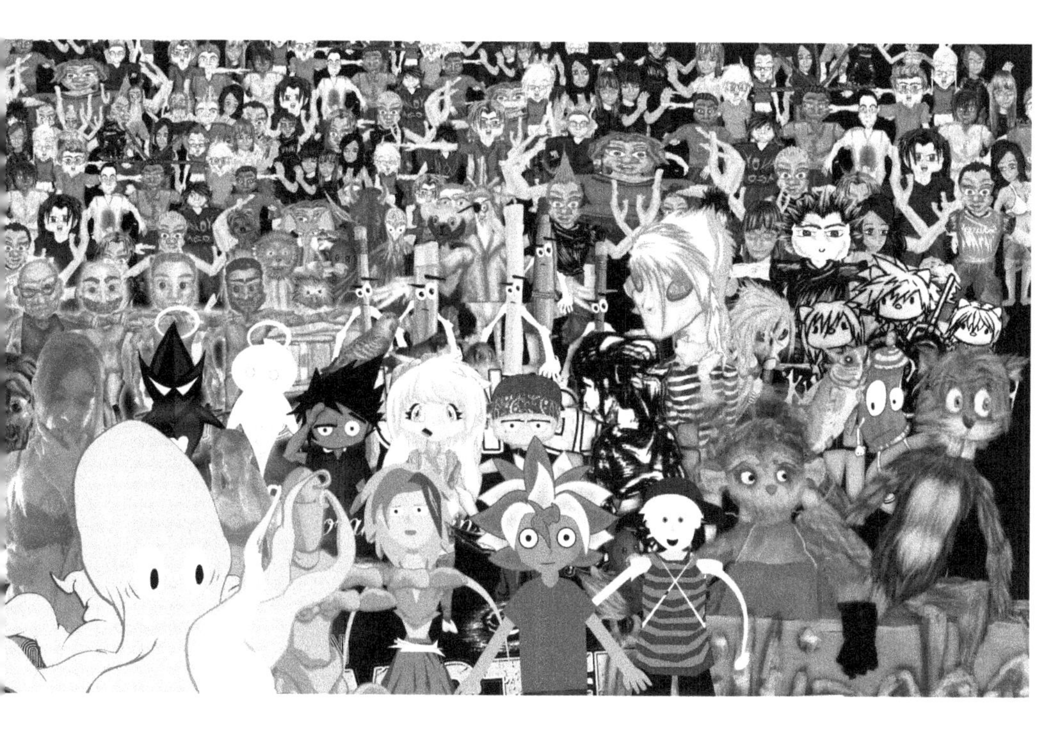

"Divinity Z"
2013
Digital

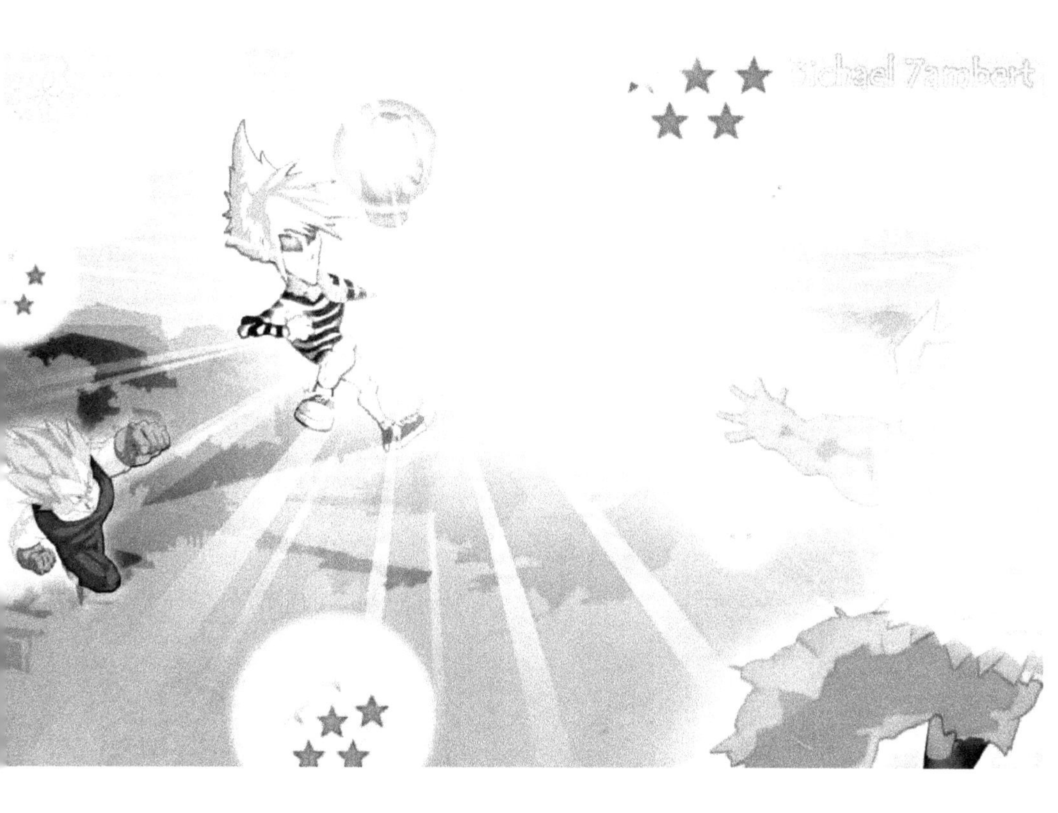

Michael Zambert

"Outerspace"
2021
Digital

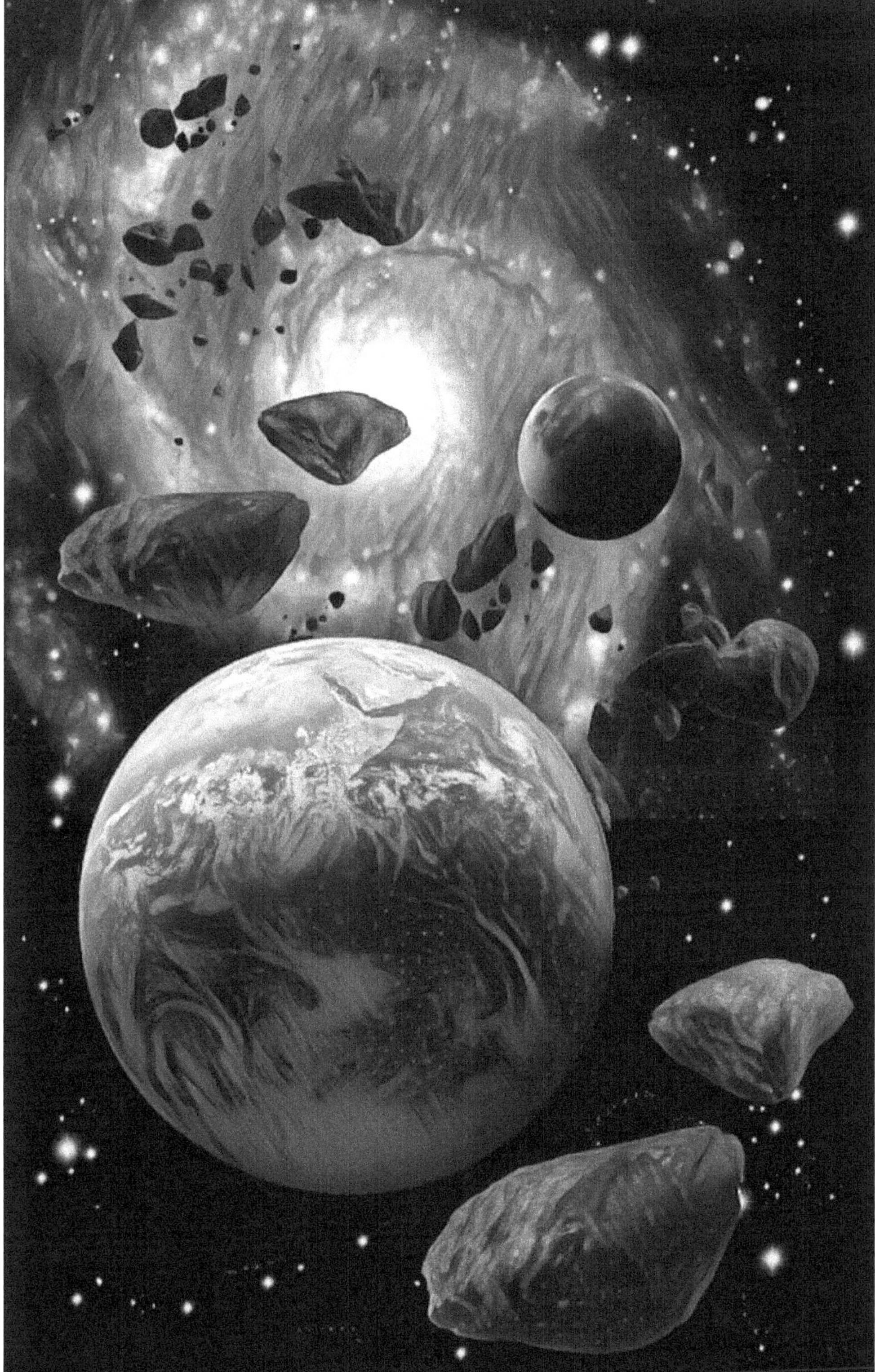

"The Dancer"
2020
Digital

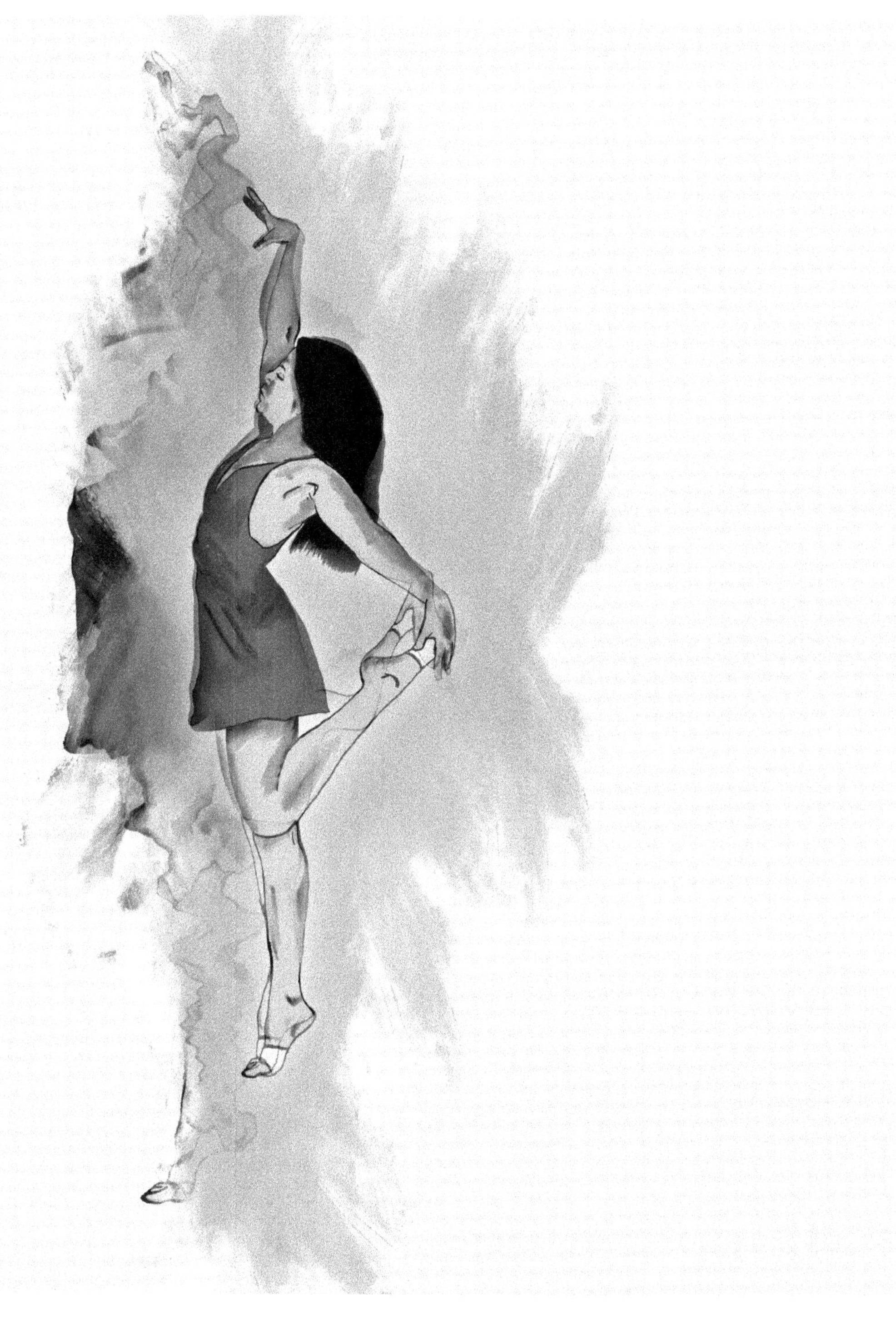

"Neon Space Girl"
2020
Digital

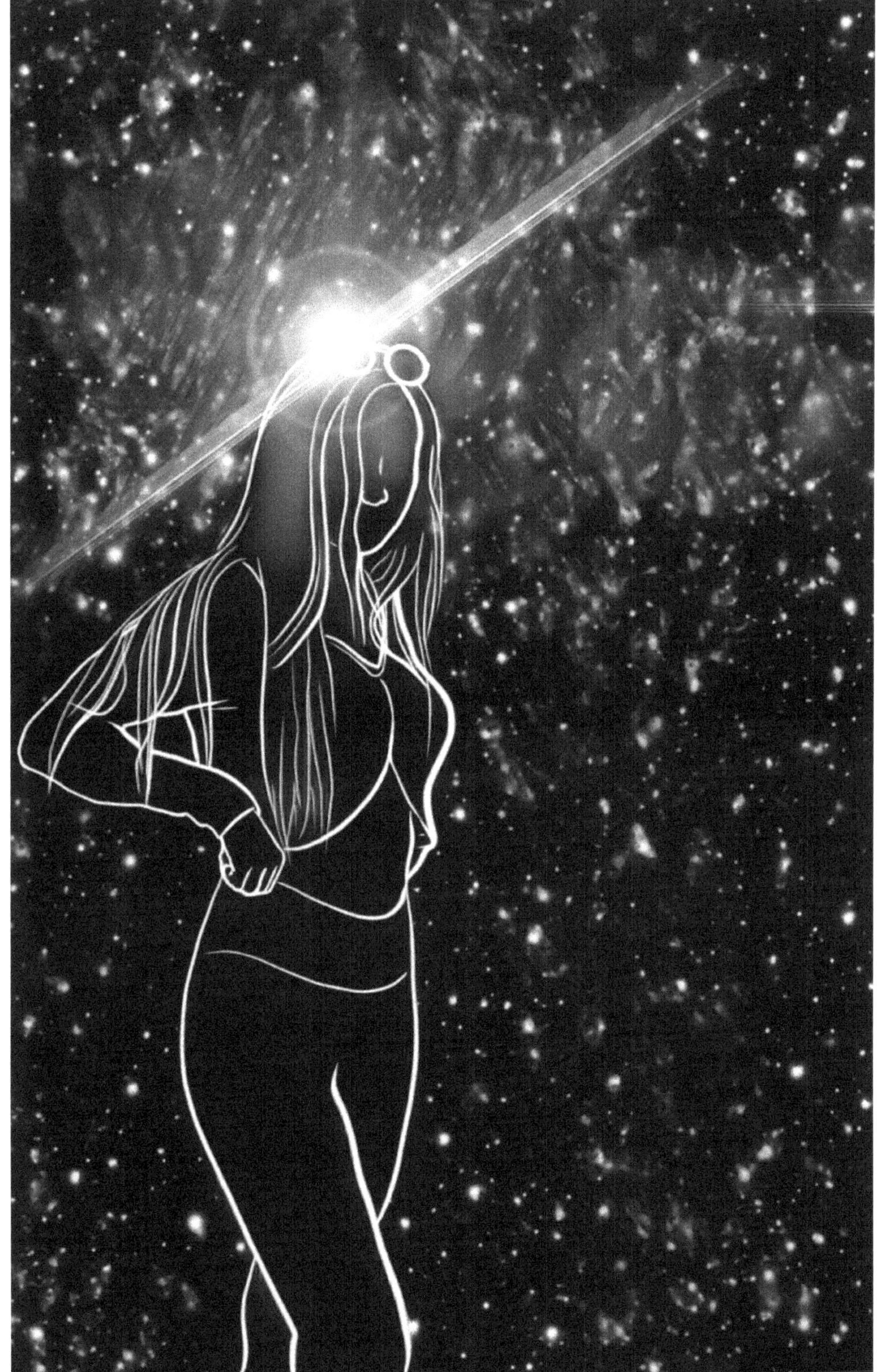

"Jellyfish"
2020
Digital

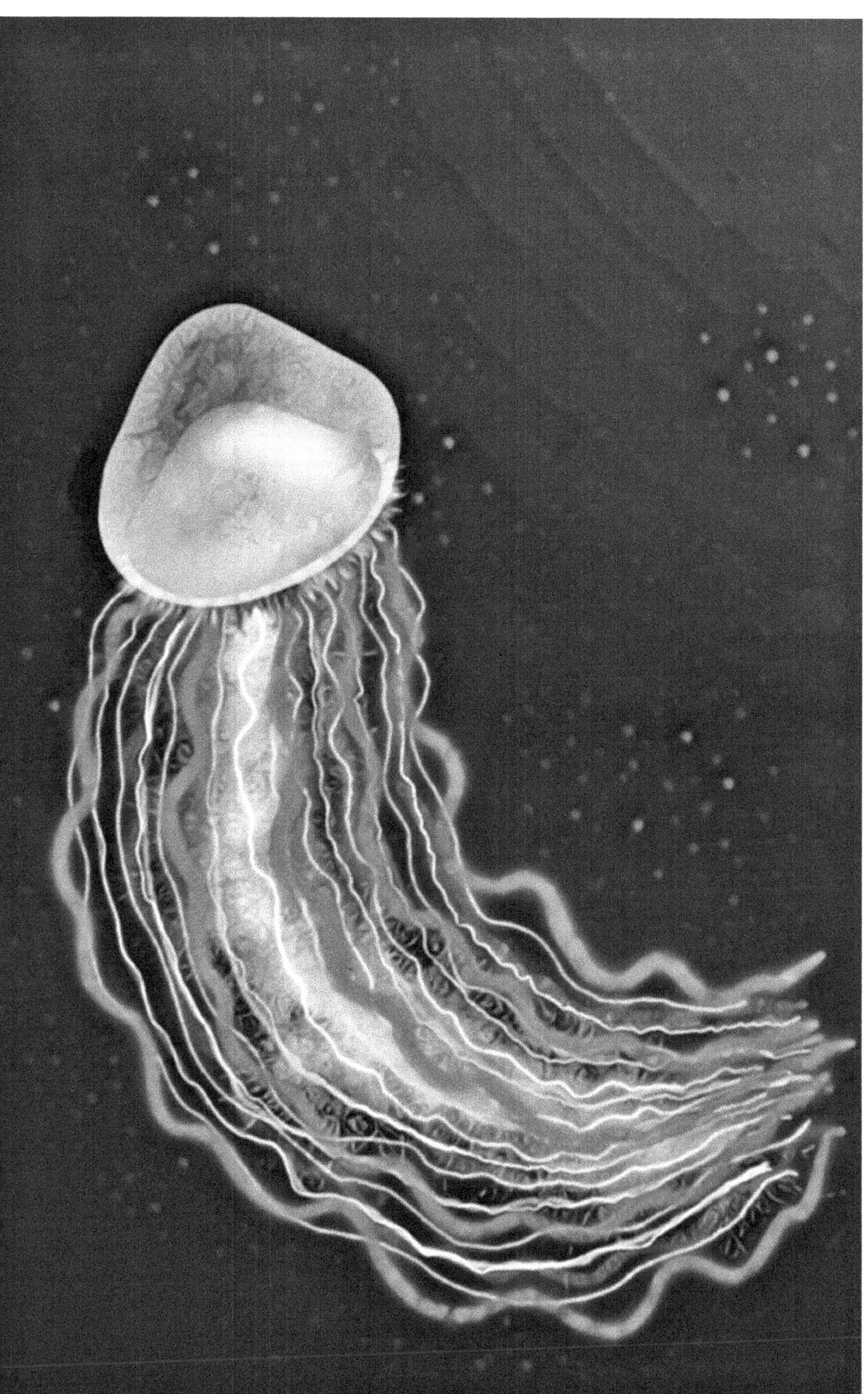

"Orbs"
2021
Digital

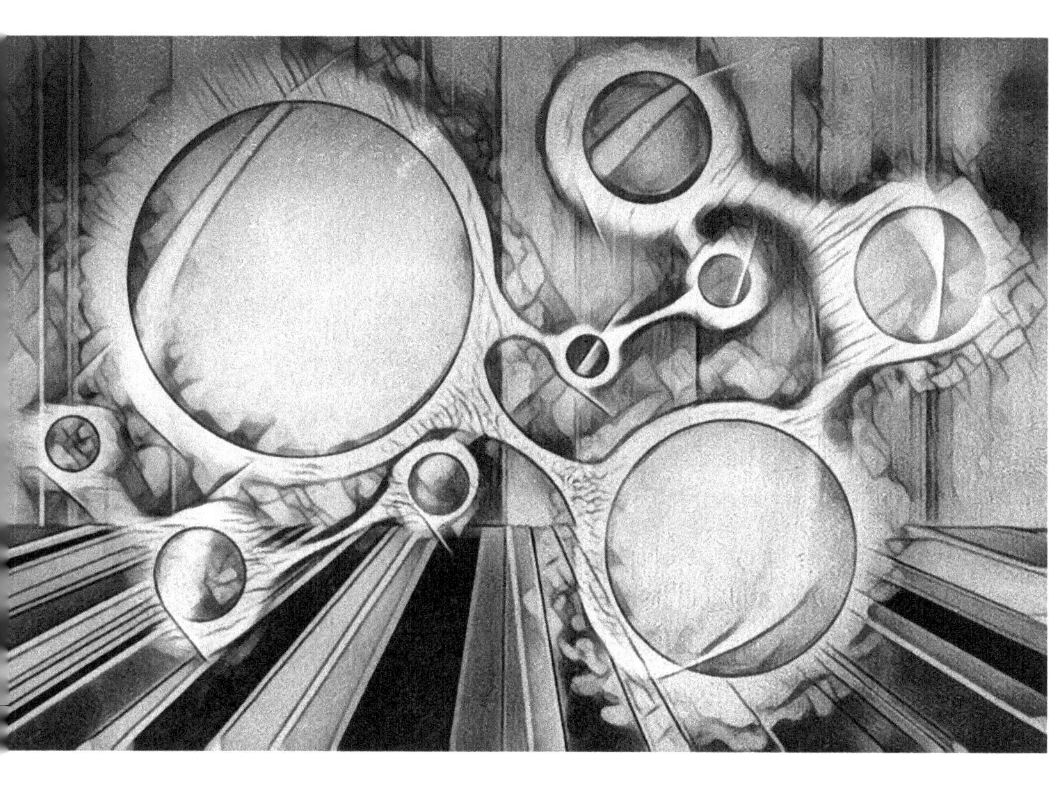

"Rubik's Comic"
2020
Digital

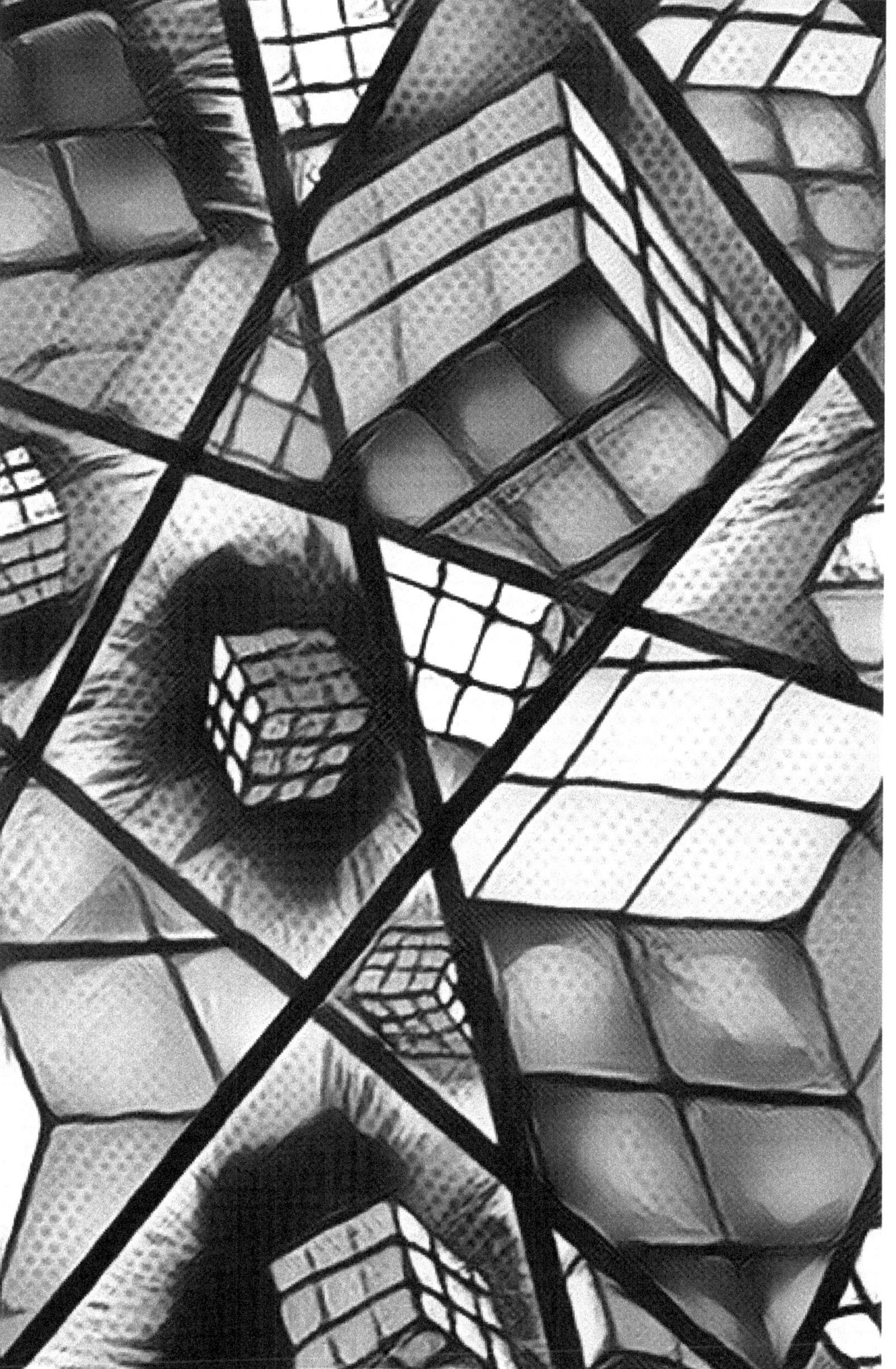

"Dragonballs"
2020
Digital

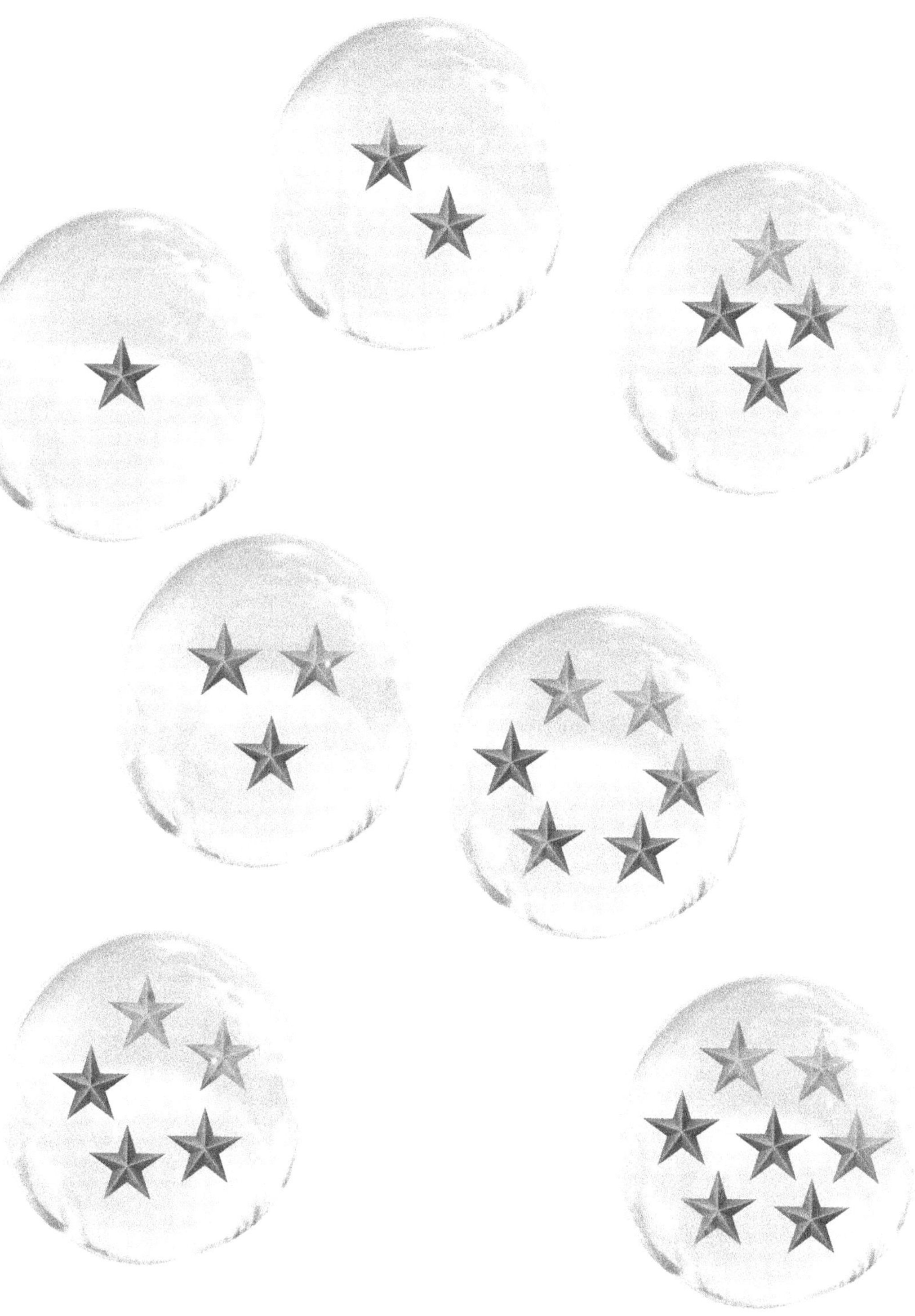

"School of Jellyfish"
2021
Digital

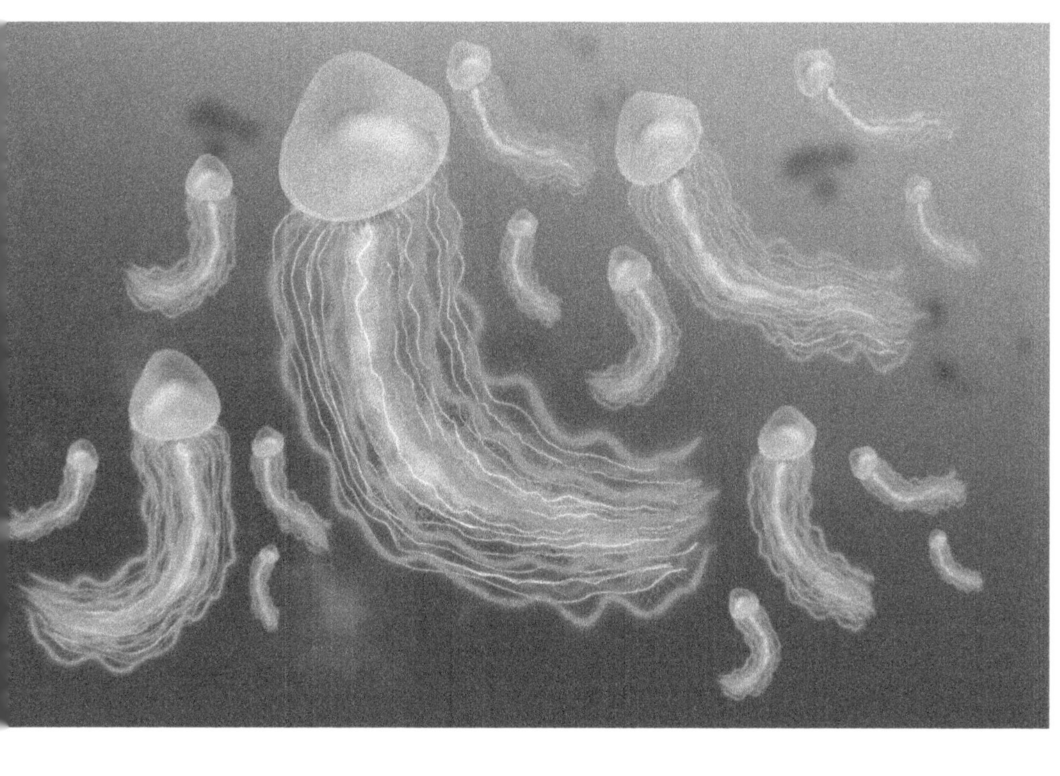

"Jellyfishes"
2020
Digital

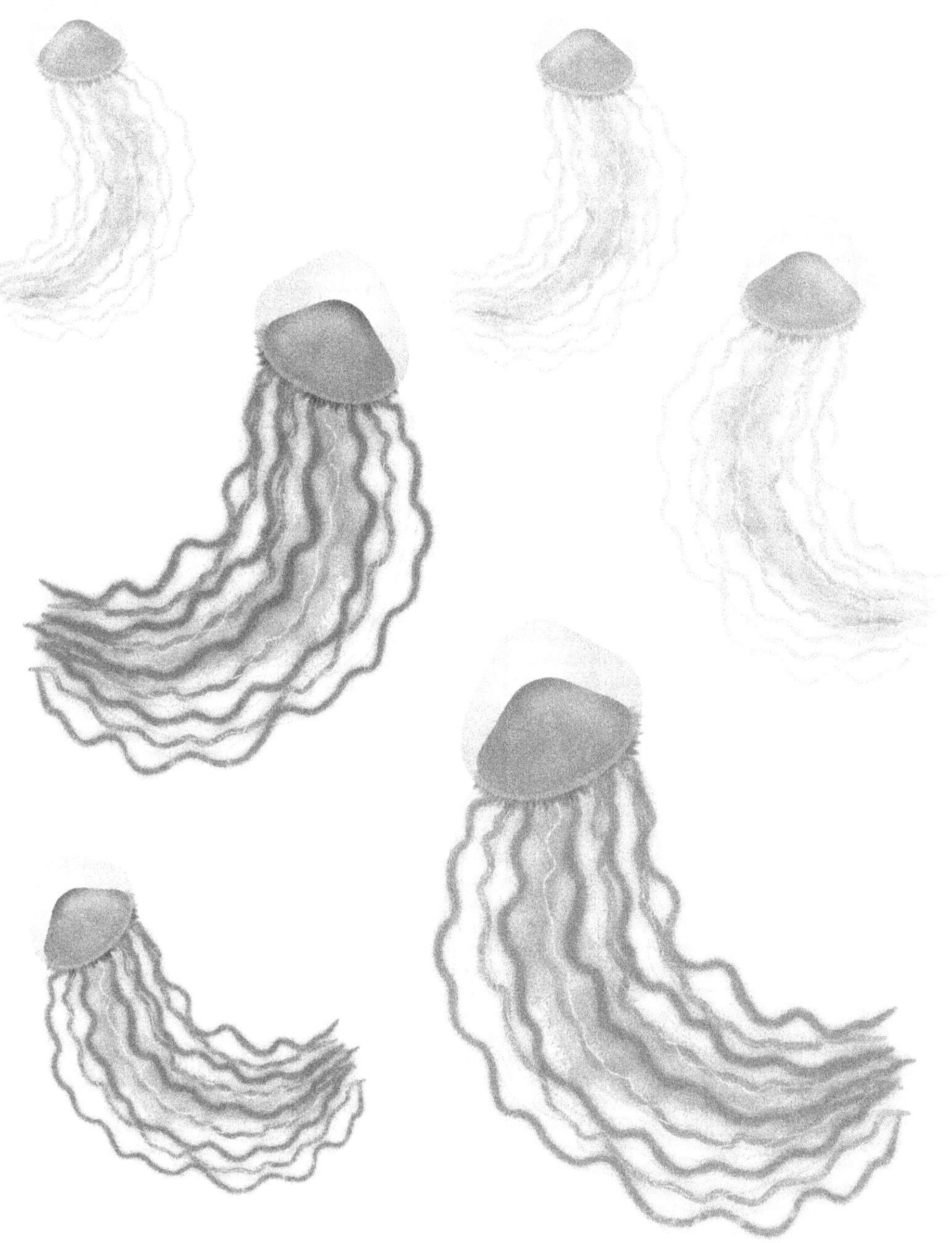

"3ichael 7ambert"
2021
Digital

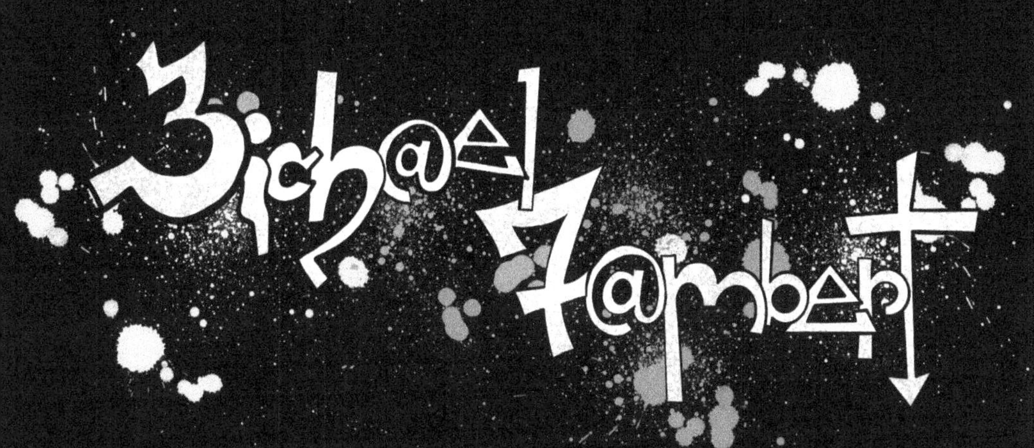
3ich@el 7ambert

"Spider Saiyan"
2020
Digital

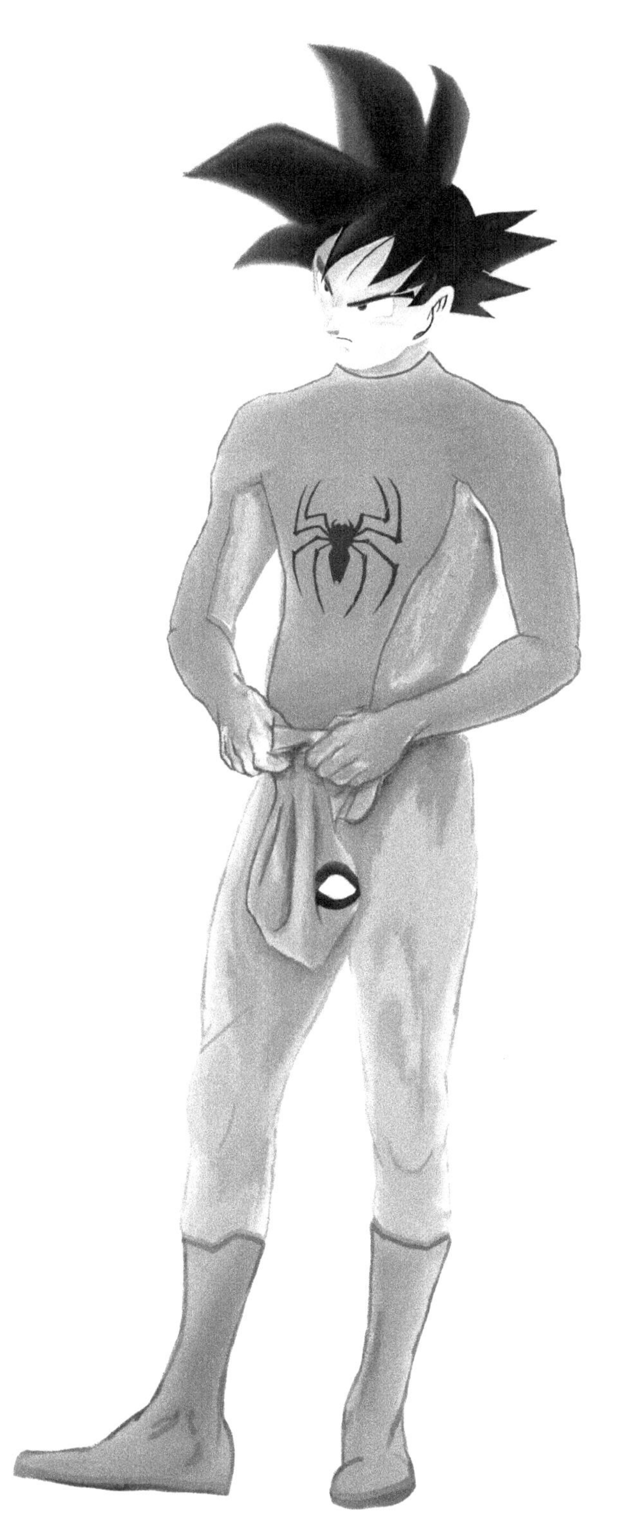

"The Paper Arcade Asteroids Promo"
2013
Game

The Paper Arcade

Asteroids

..Ind'd Out Edition

"Alien Ocean"
2018
Digital

"Dark Lake"
2018
Digital

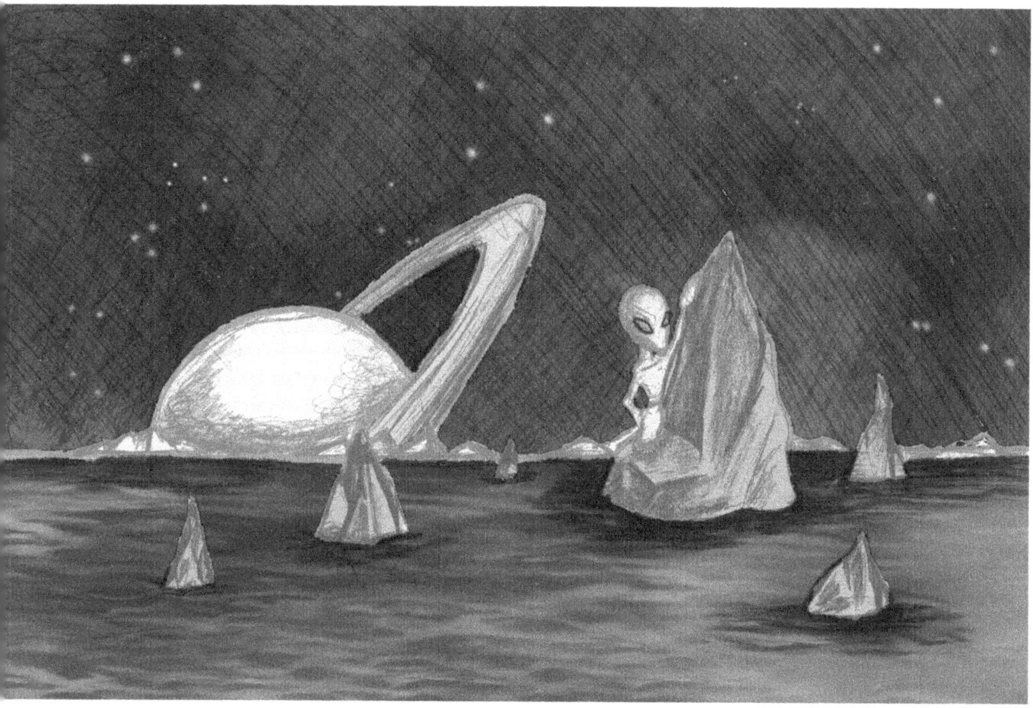

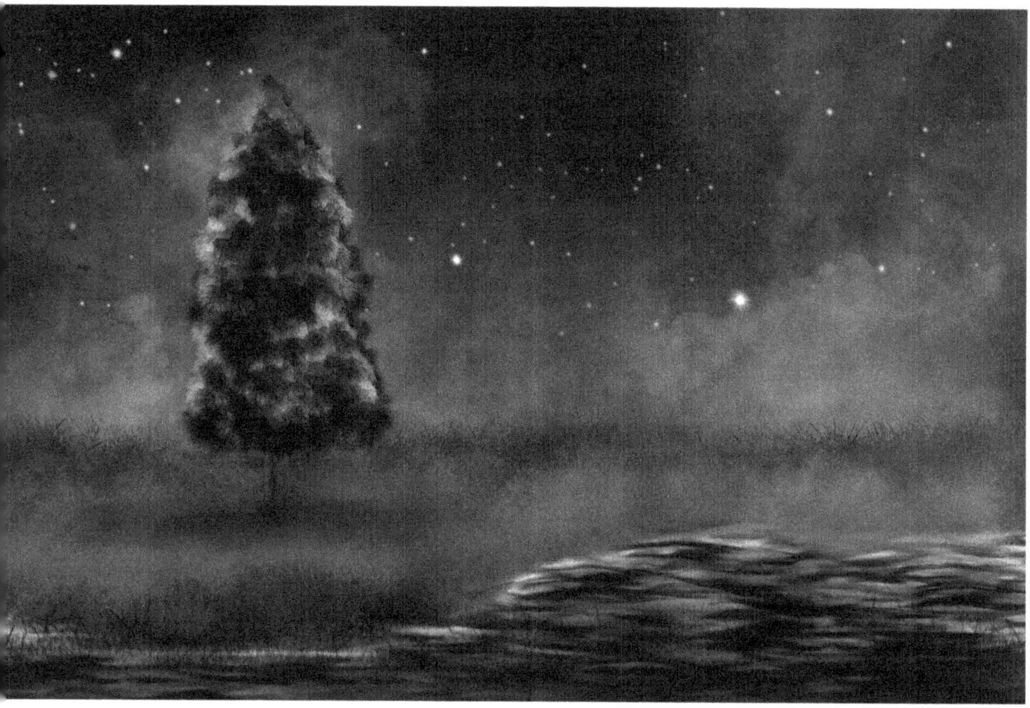

"Relax"
2017
Digital Ink

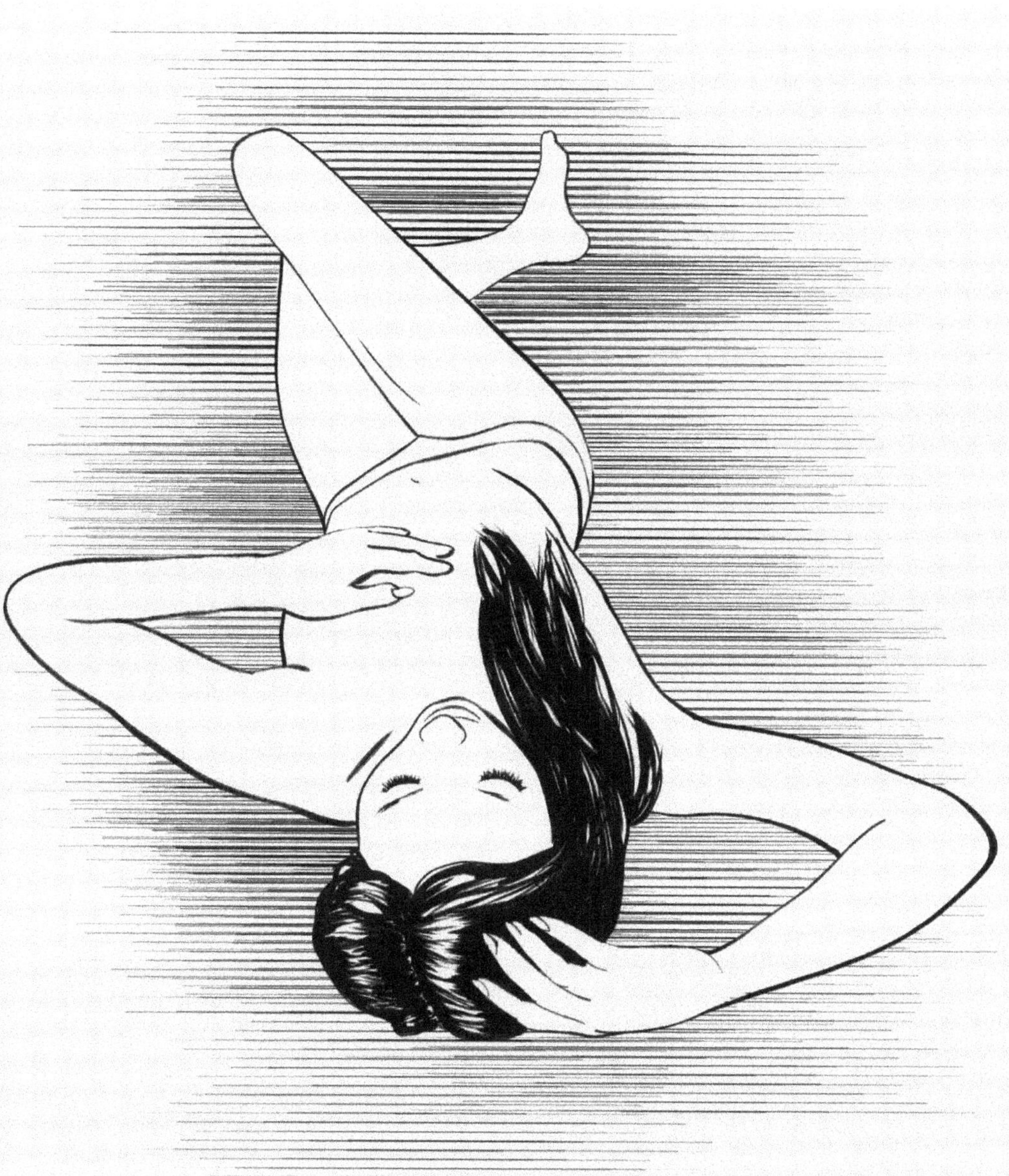

"Danny"
2020
Digital

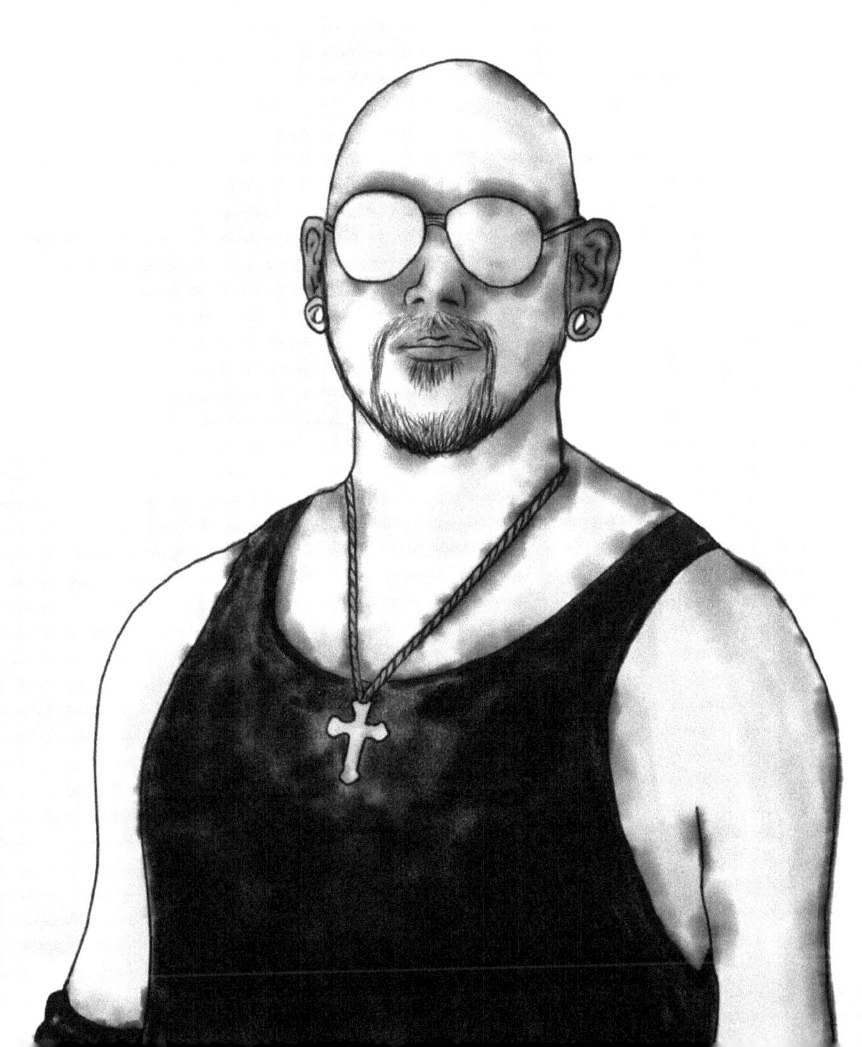

"Little Vacation"
2021
Digital

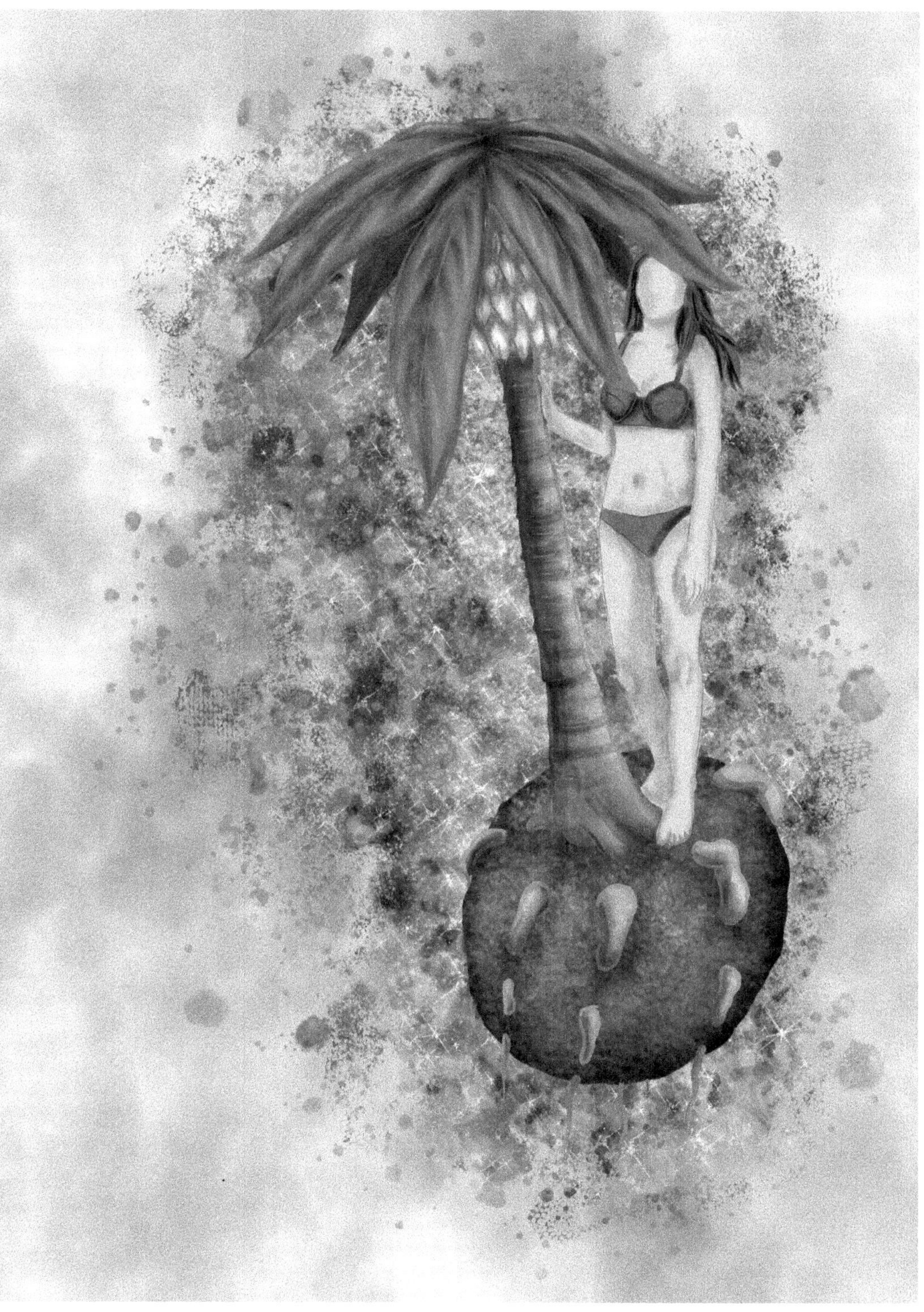

"Heading to Vacay"
2021
Digital

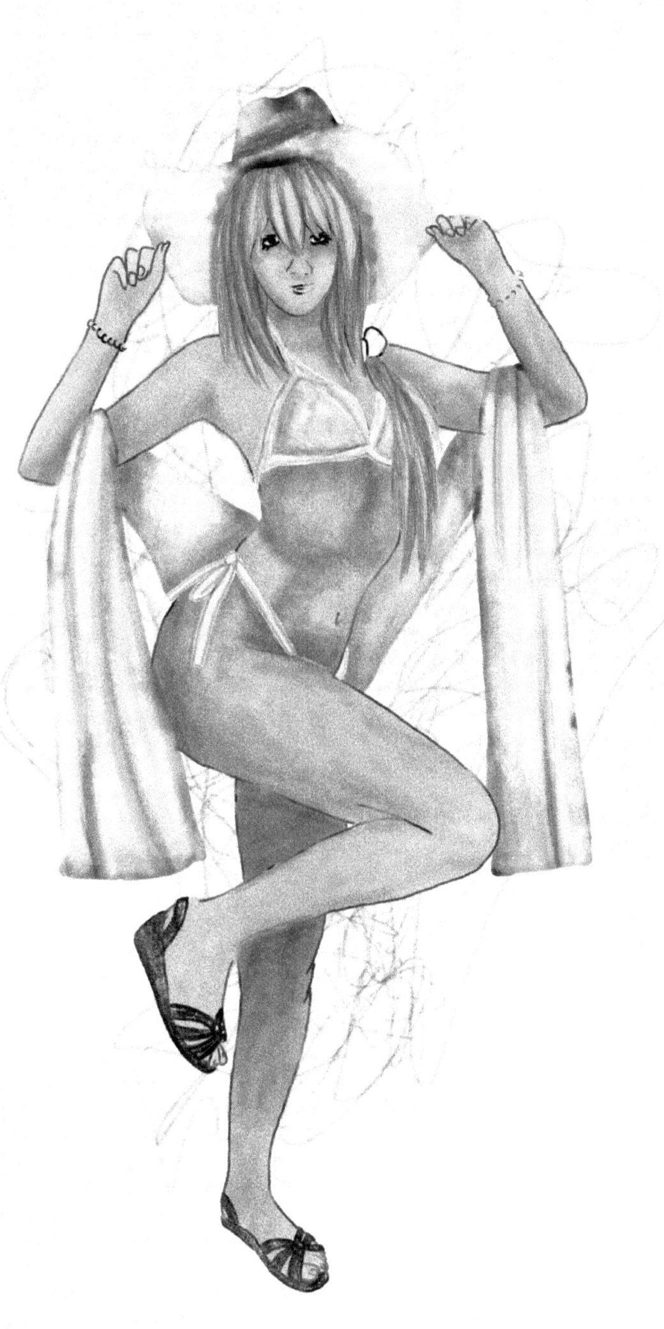

"Newspaper Lady"
2021
Digital Ink

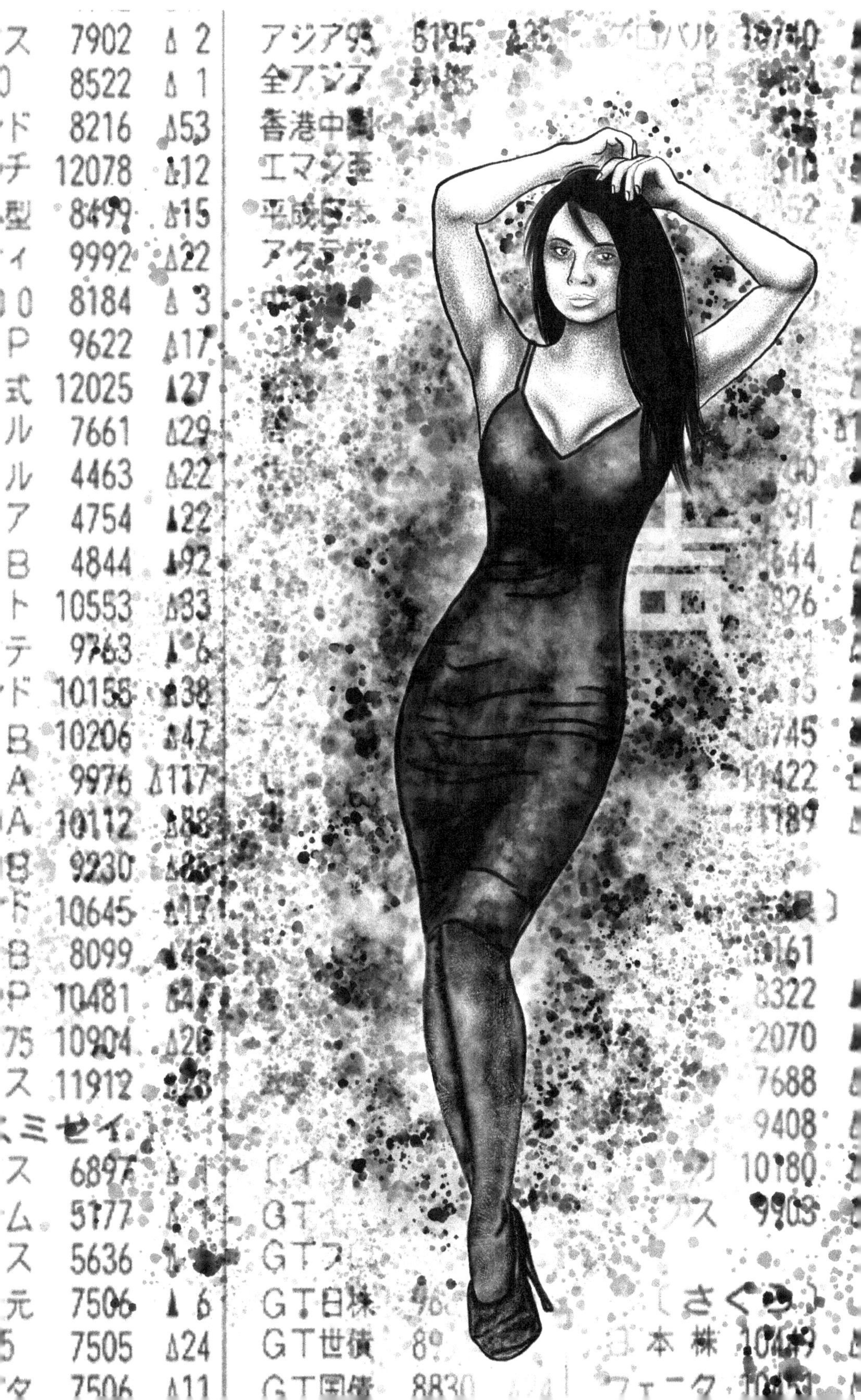

"Bunny Girl"
2021
Digital

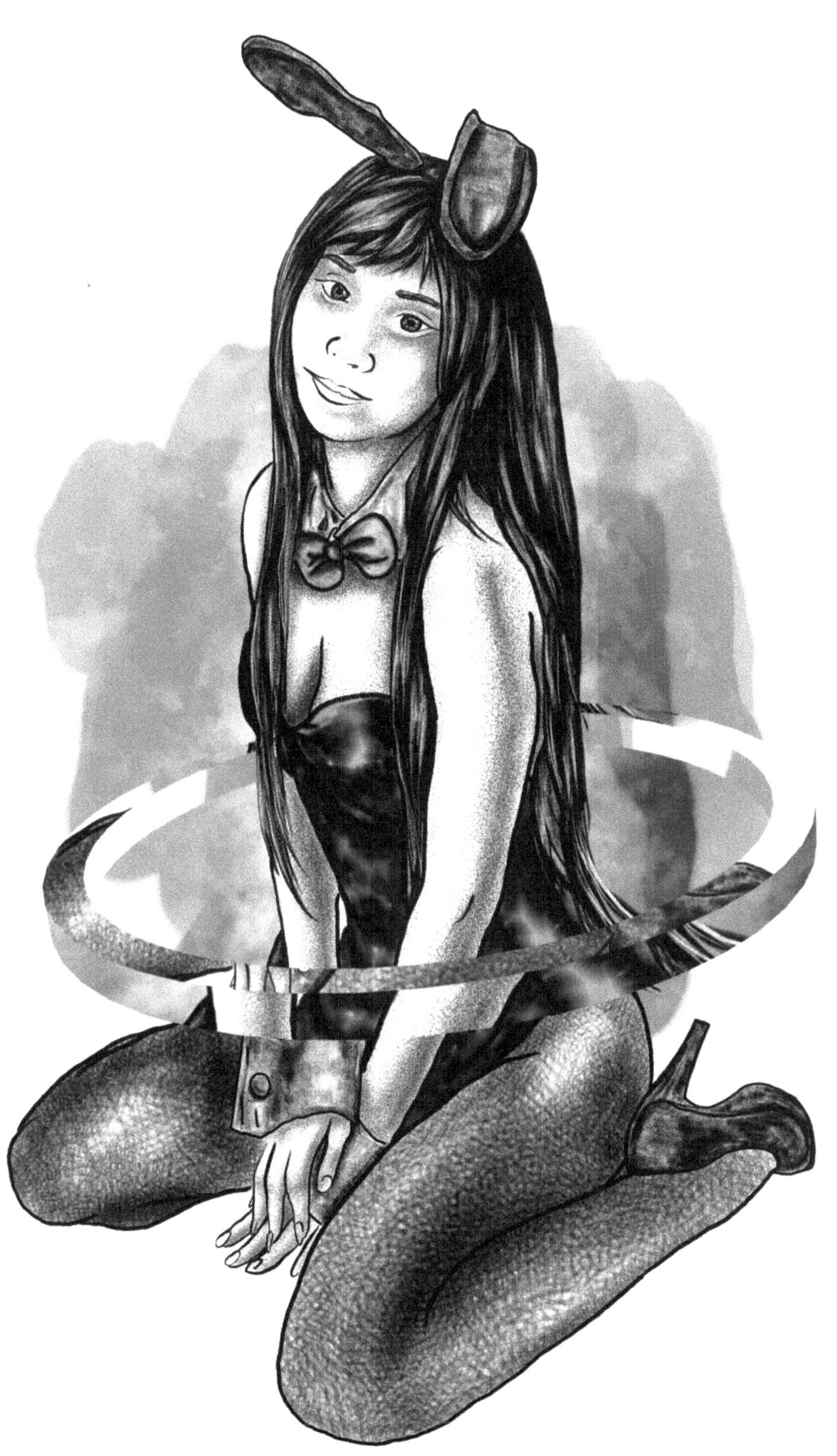

"Girl in Bubble"
2022
Digital

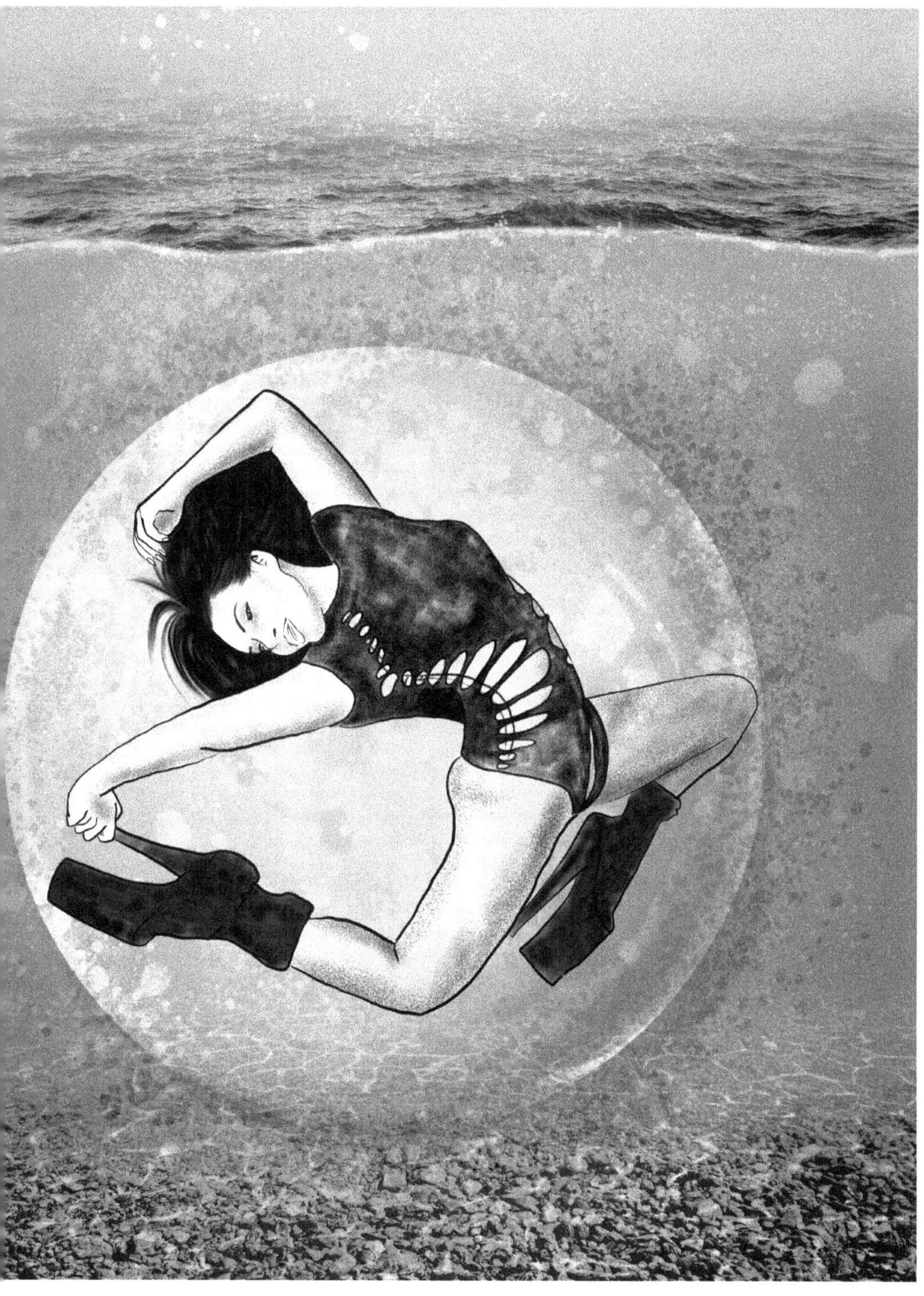

"Portraitography: The Female Figure"
2024
Digital Ink

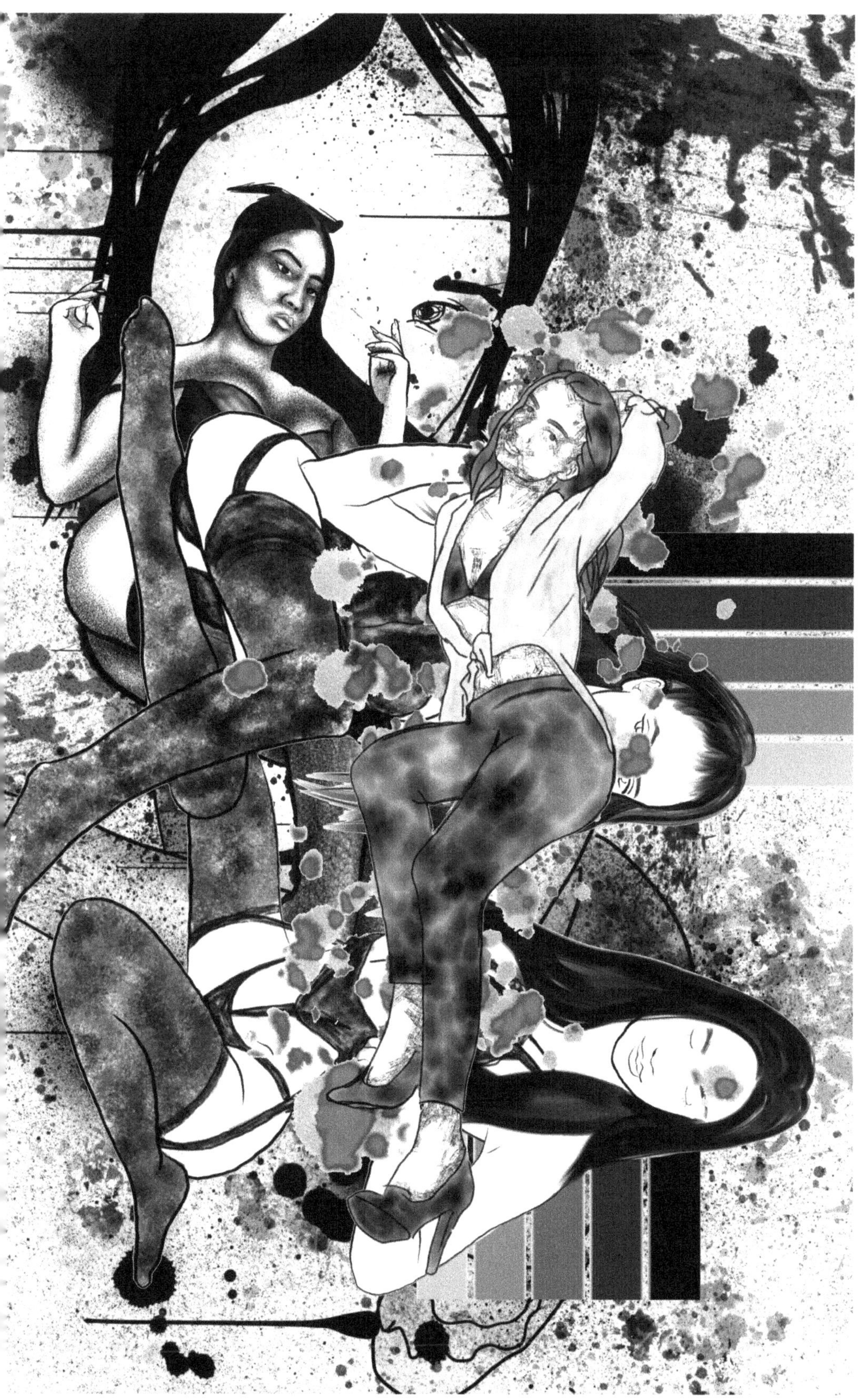

"Cherries"
2019
Digital

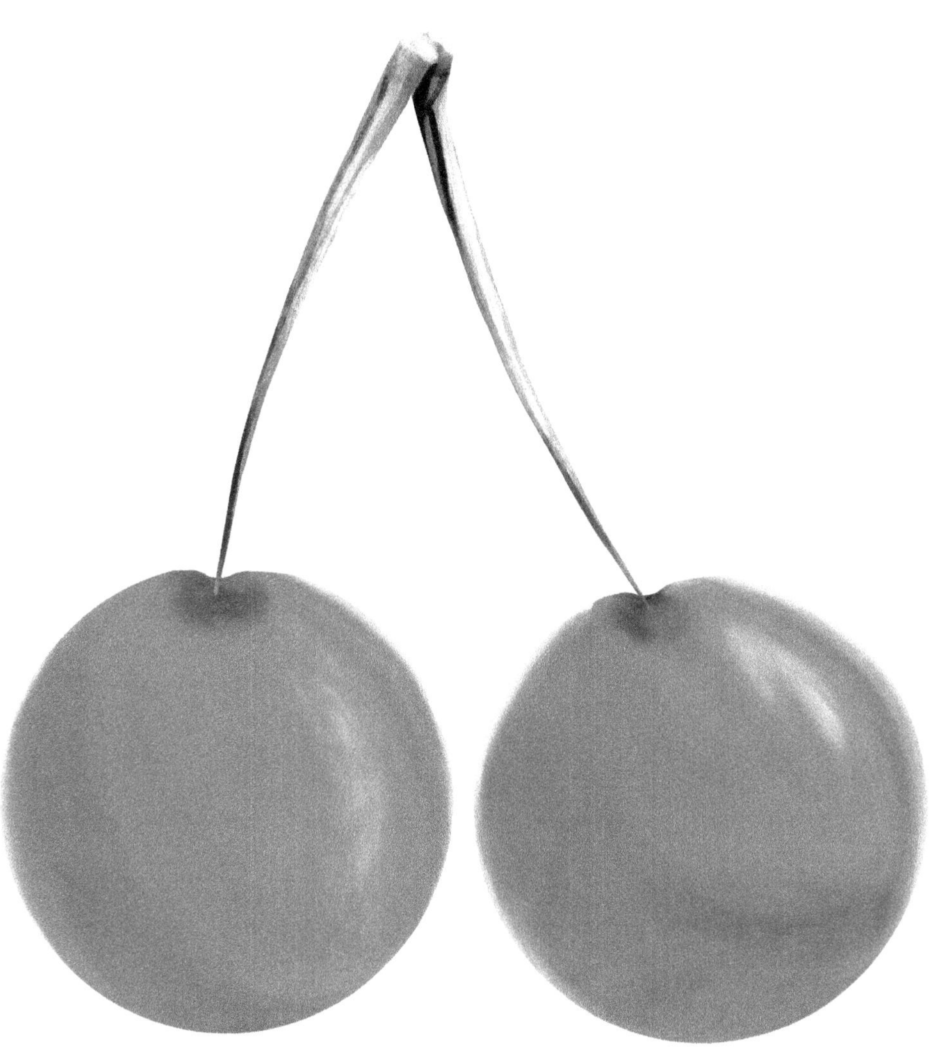

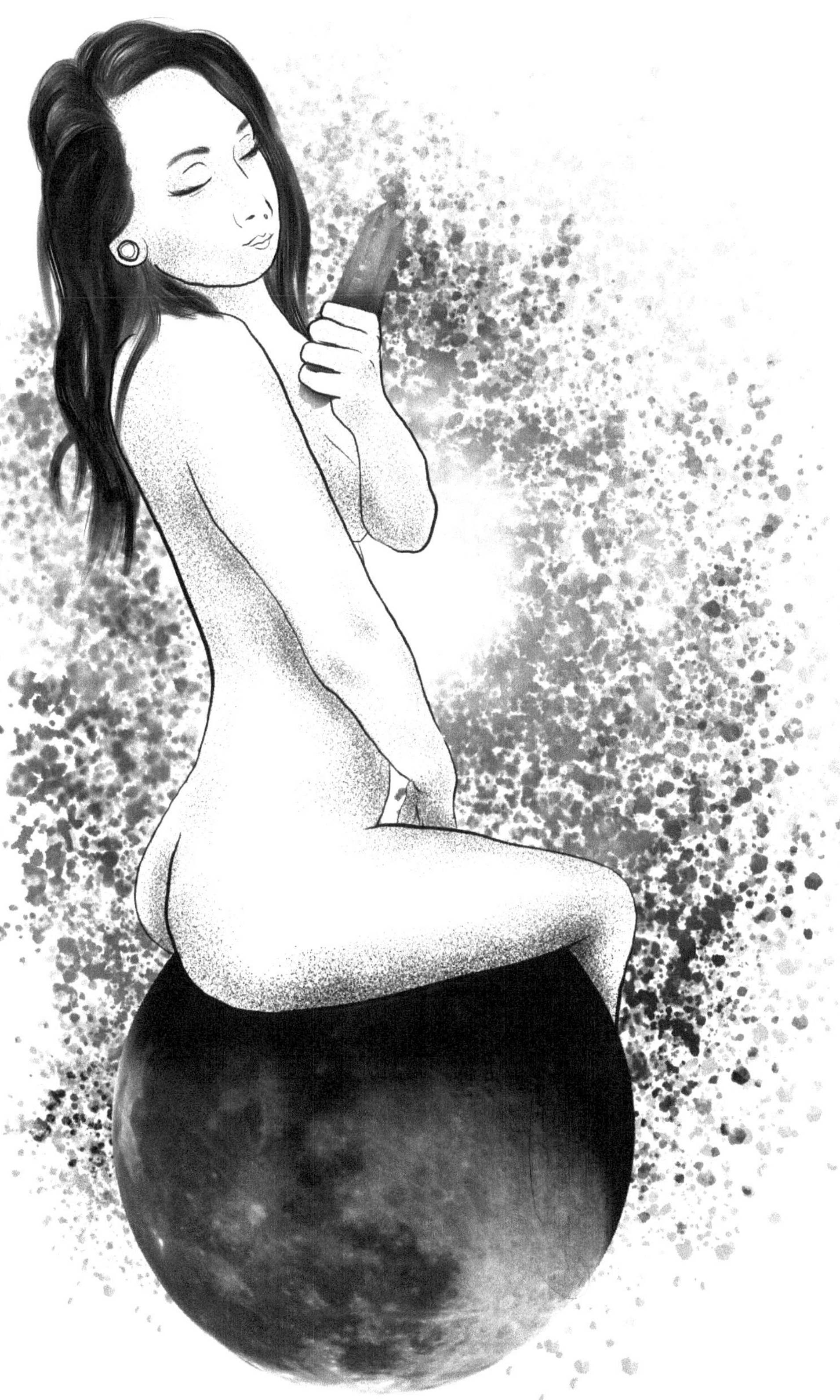

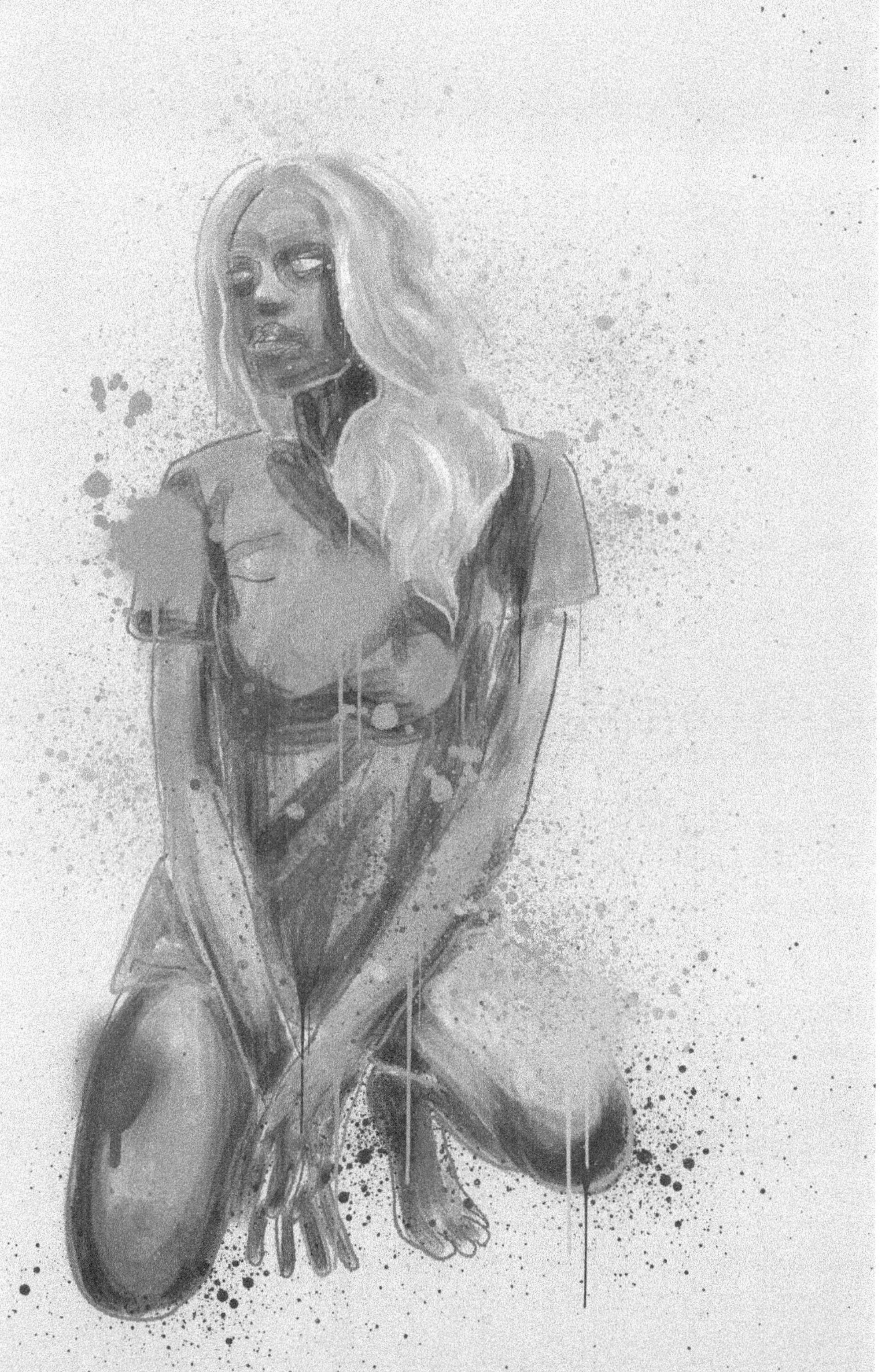

"Graffiti Girl #Purple"
2021
Digital

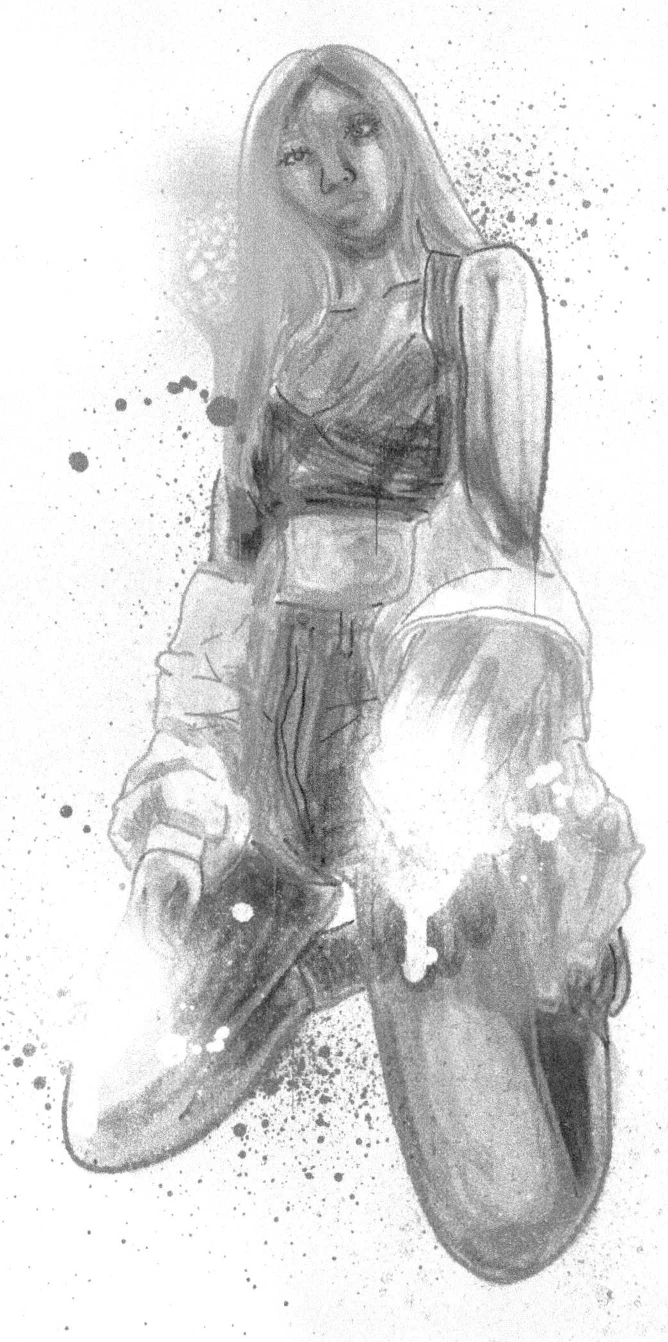

"Tucker"
2011
Egg and Marker

"Nick"
2011
Egg and Marker

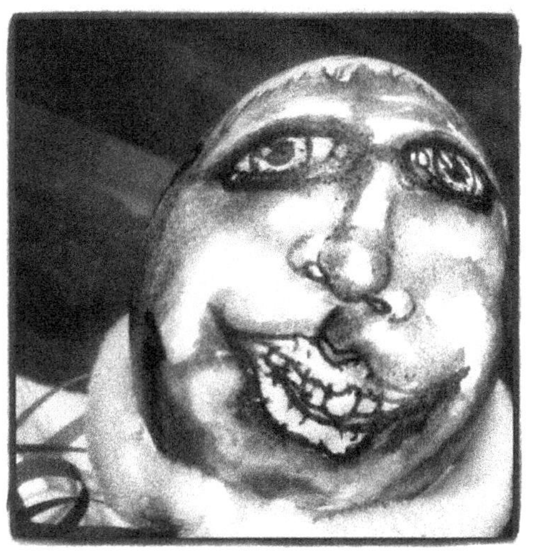
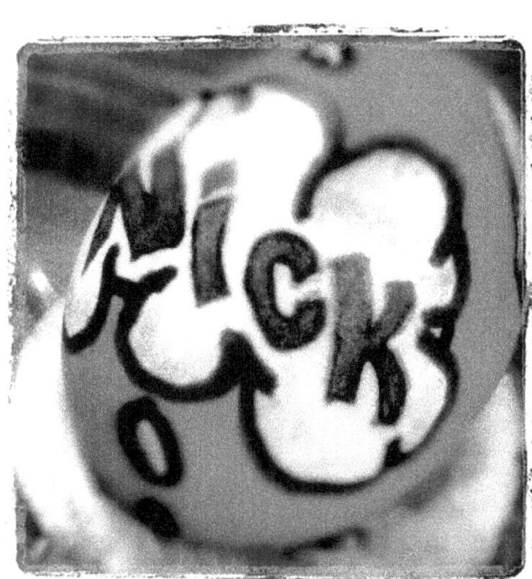
iCK
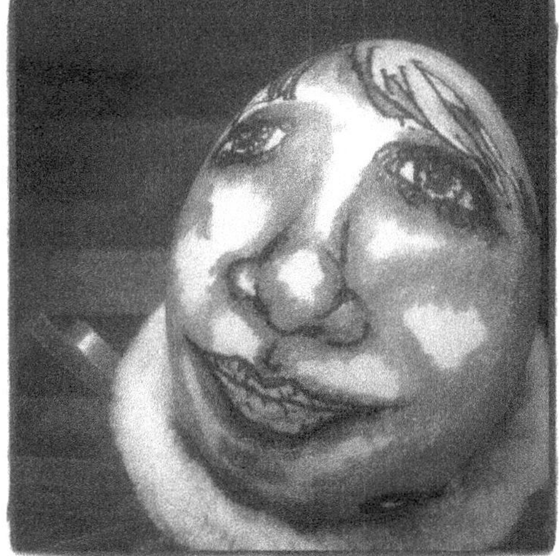
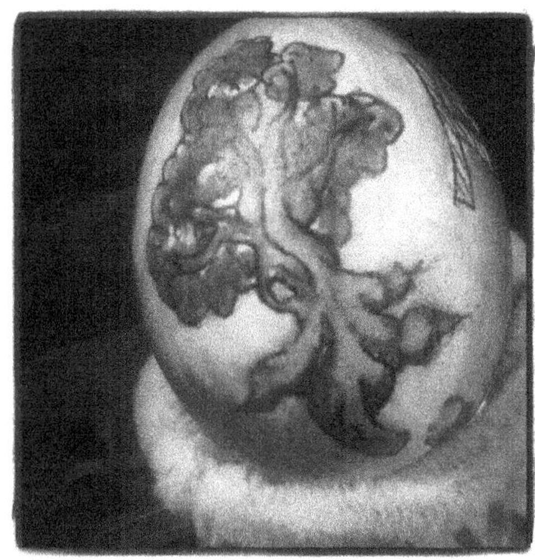

"A Rocket's Intensity Logo"
2010
Digital

"Think About It Later #Blue"
2010
Digital

"Think About It Later #Neon"
2010
Digital

"Think About It Later #Black"
2010
Digita

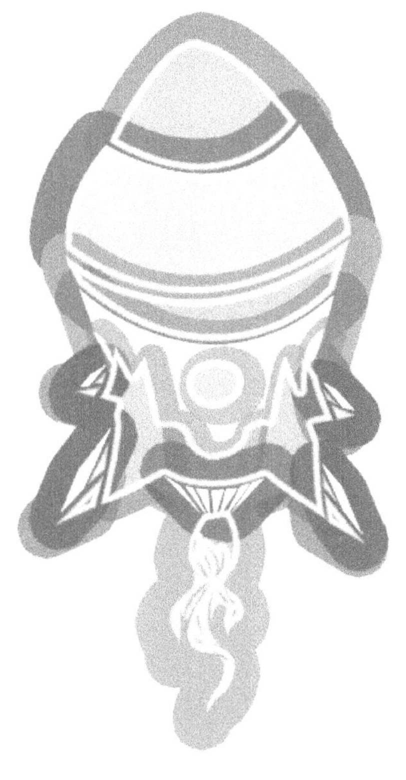

THINK ABOUT IT LATER

ThinkAboutITLater

THINK ABOUT IT LATER

myspace.com/thinkaboutitlatermusic

"Bearded Dragon #1"
2018
Photography

"Bearded Dragon #"
2018
Photography

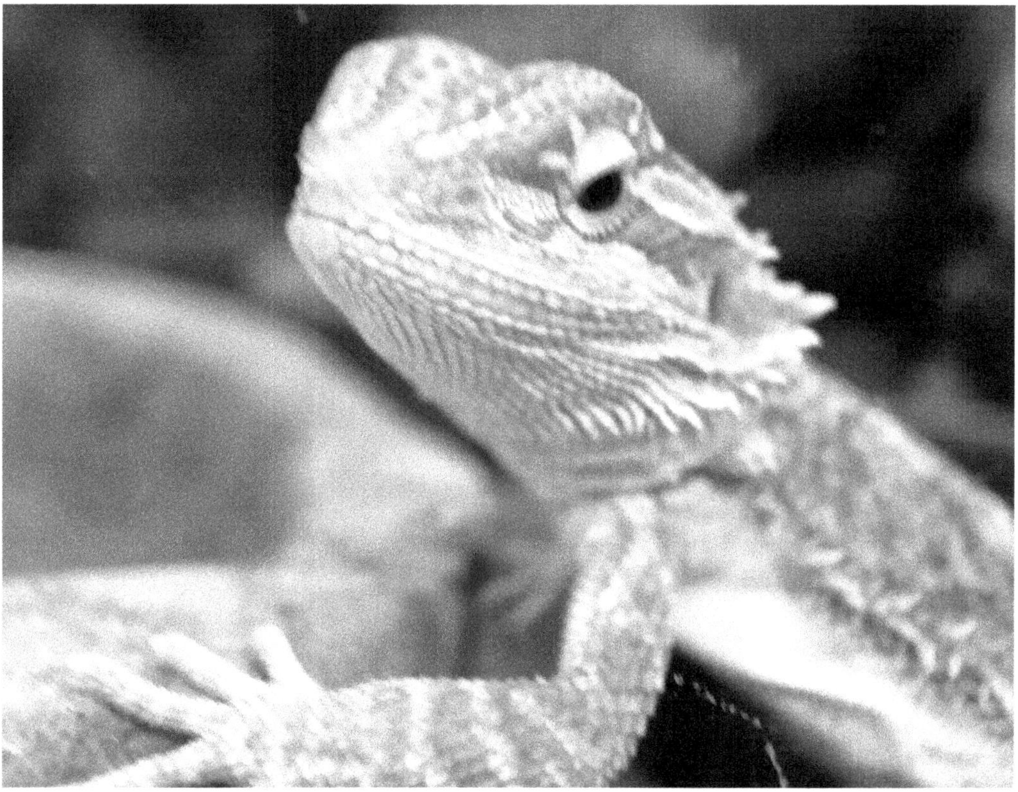

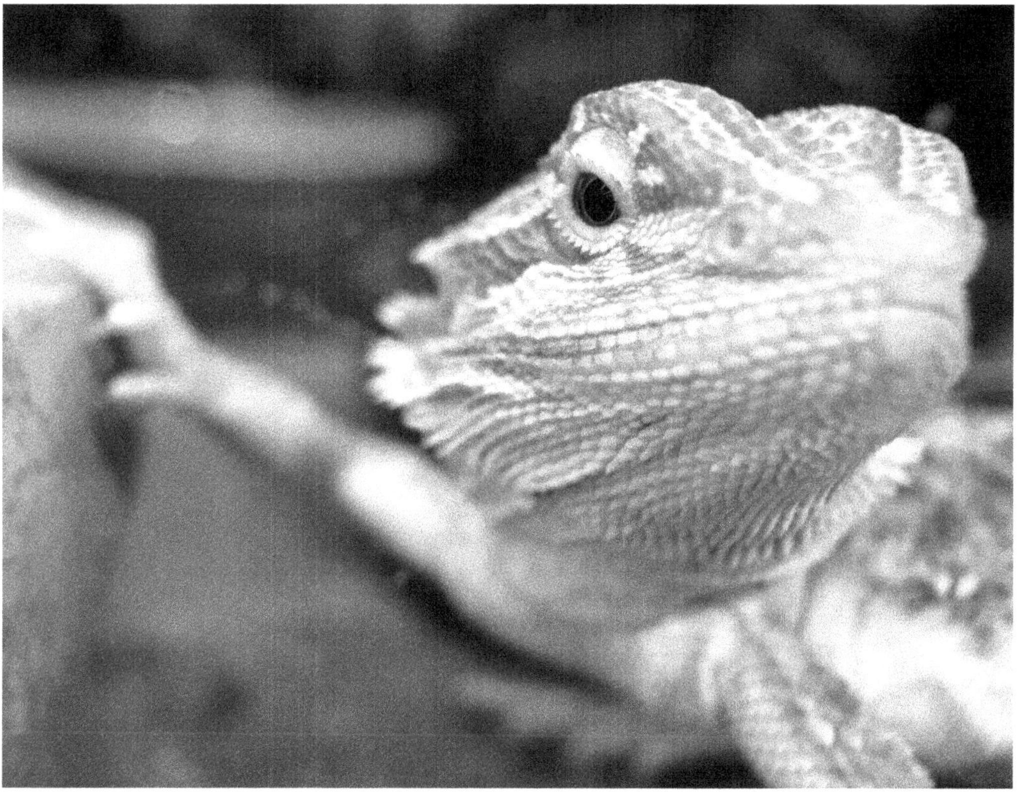

"The Green Planet"
2019
360 Photography

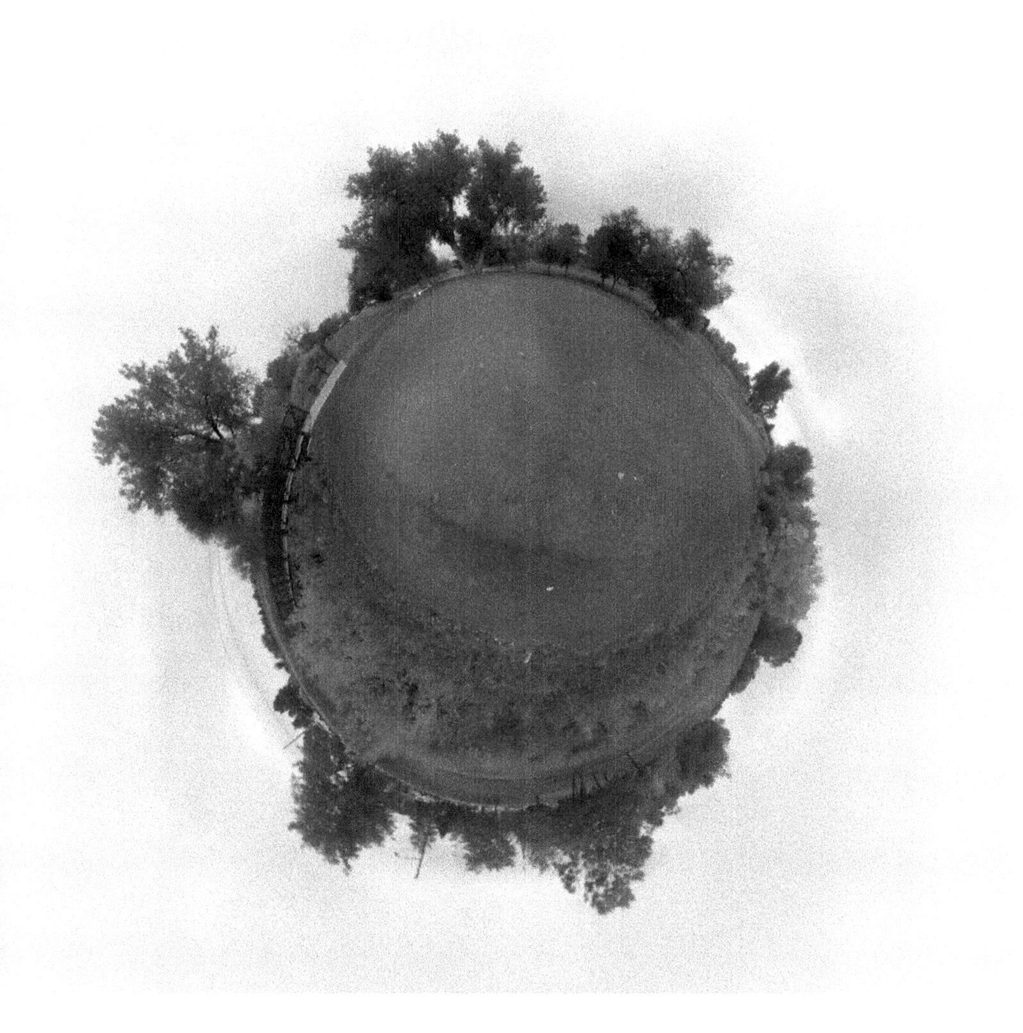

"Samurai Girl"
2021
Digital

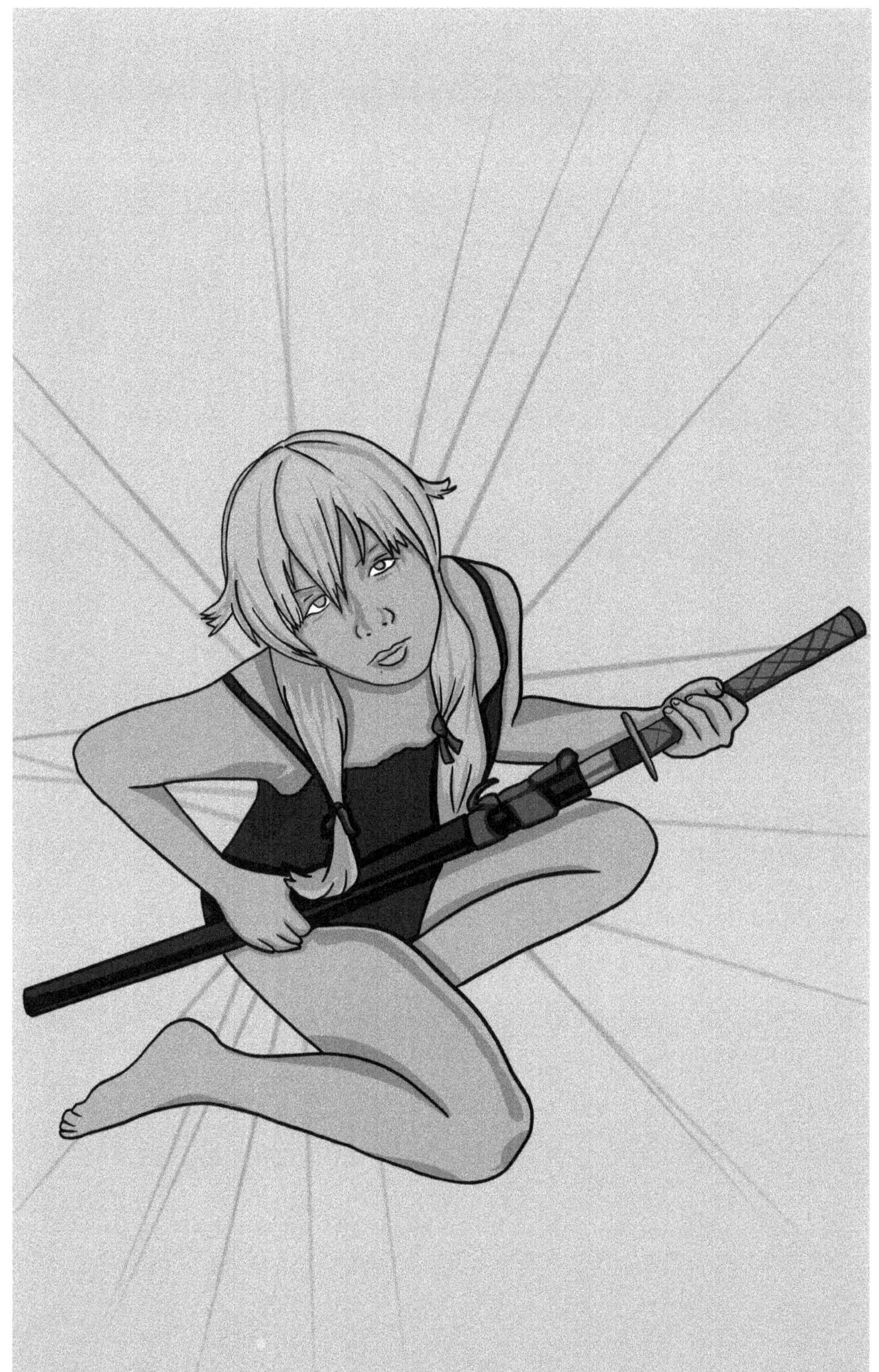

"Neon Swag"
2021
Digital

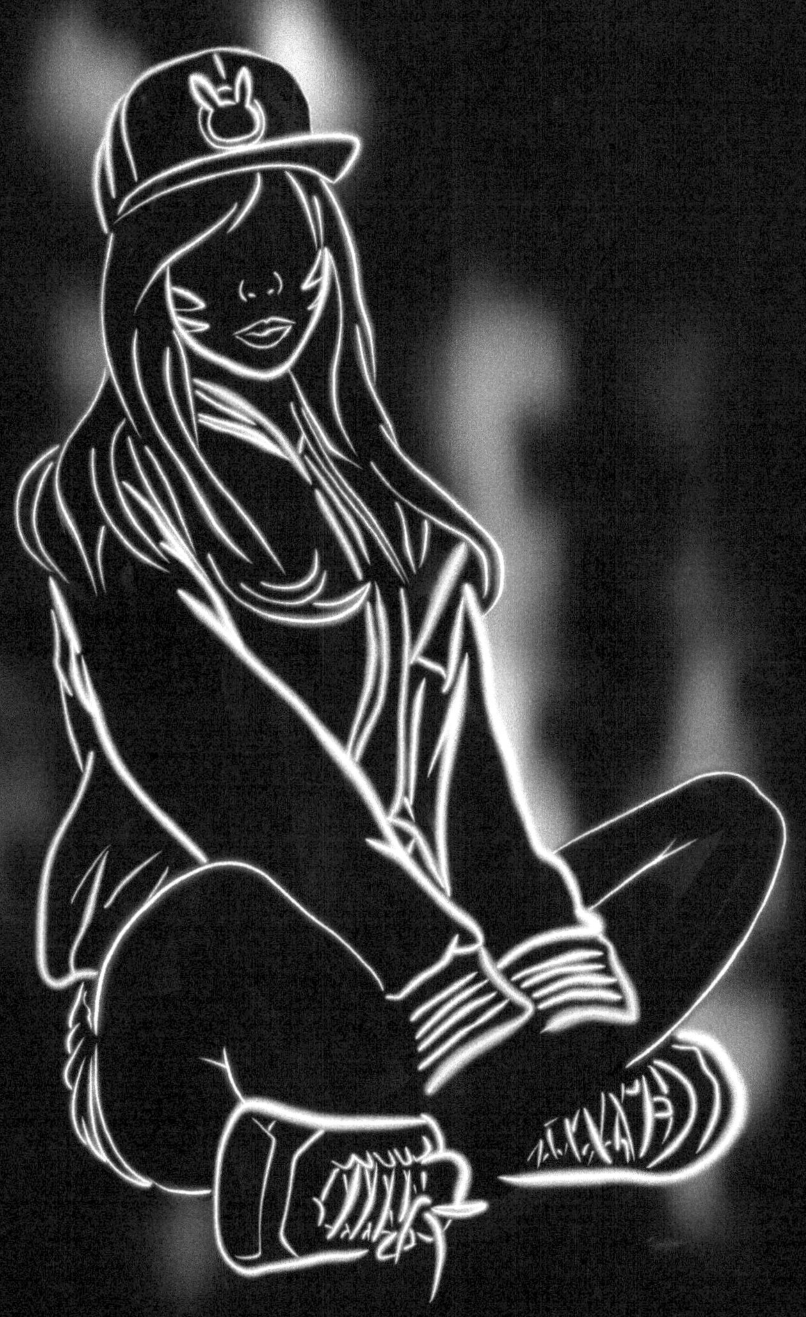

"Urban Girl"
2021
Digital

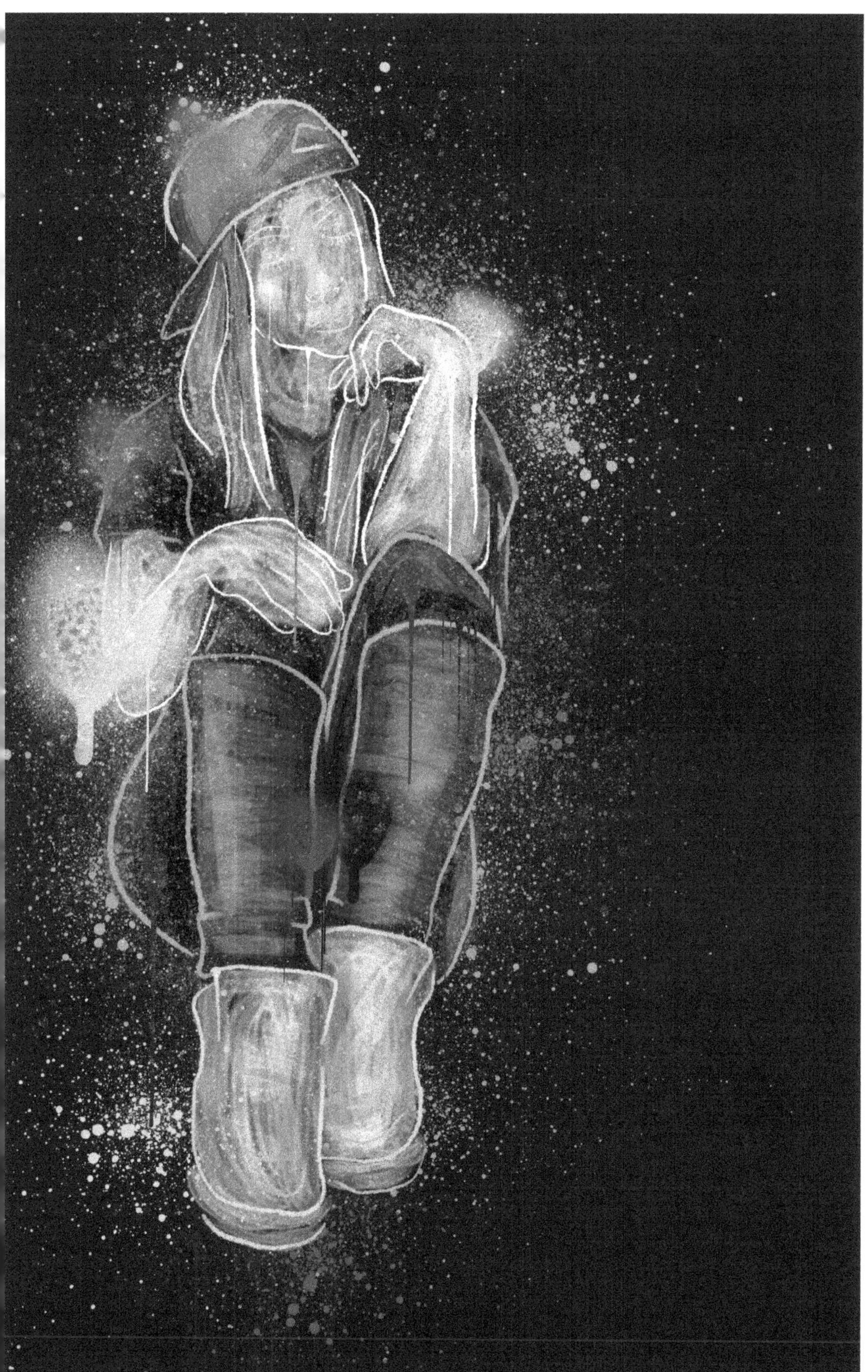

"Fall From Heaven"
2021
Digital

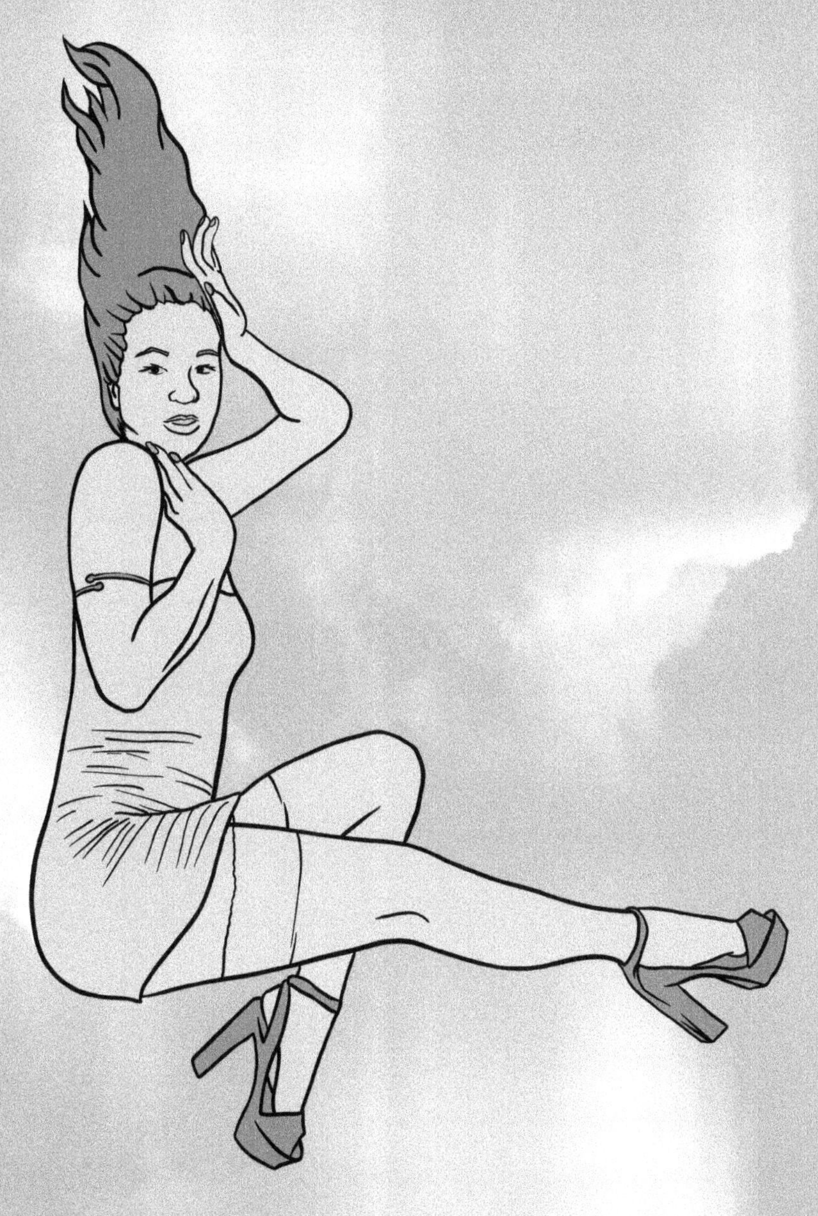

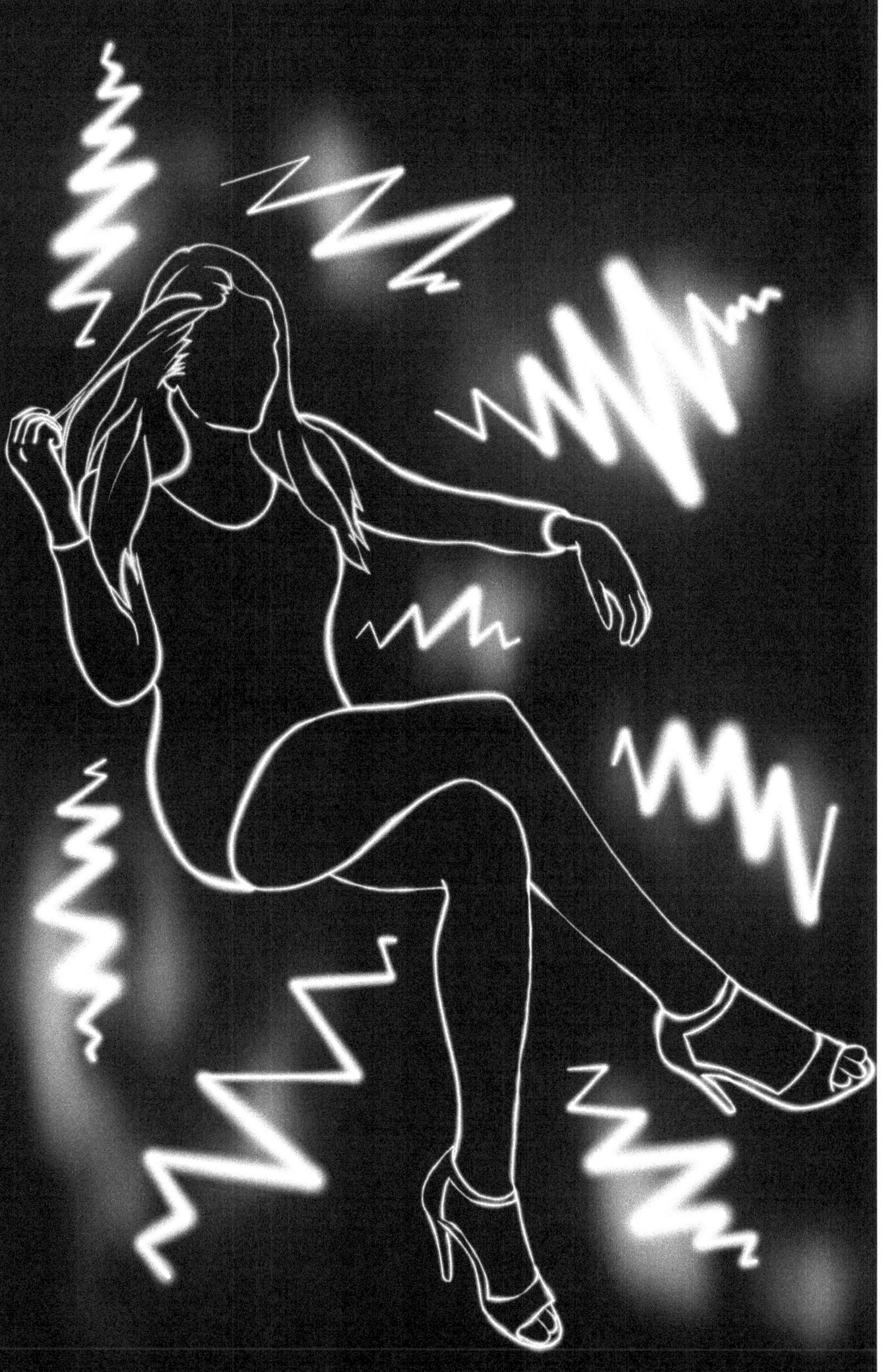

"Yoga"
2021
Markers

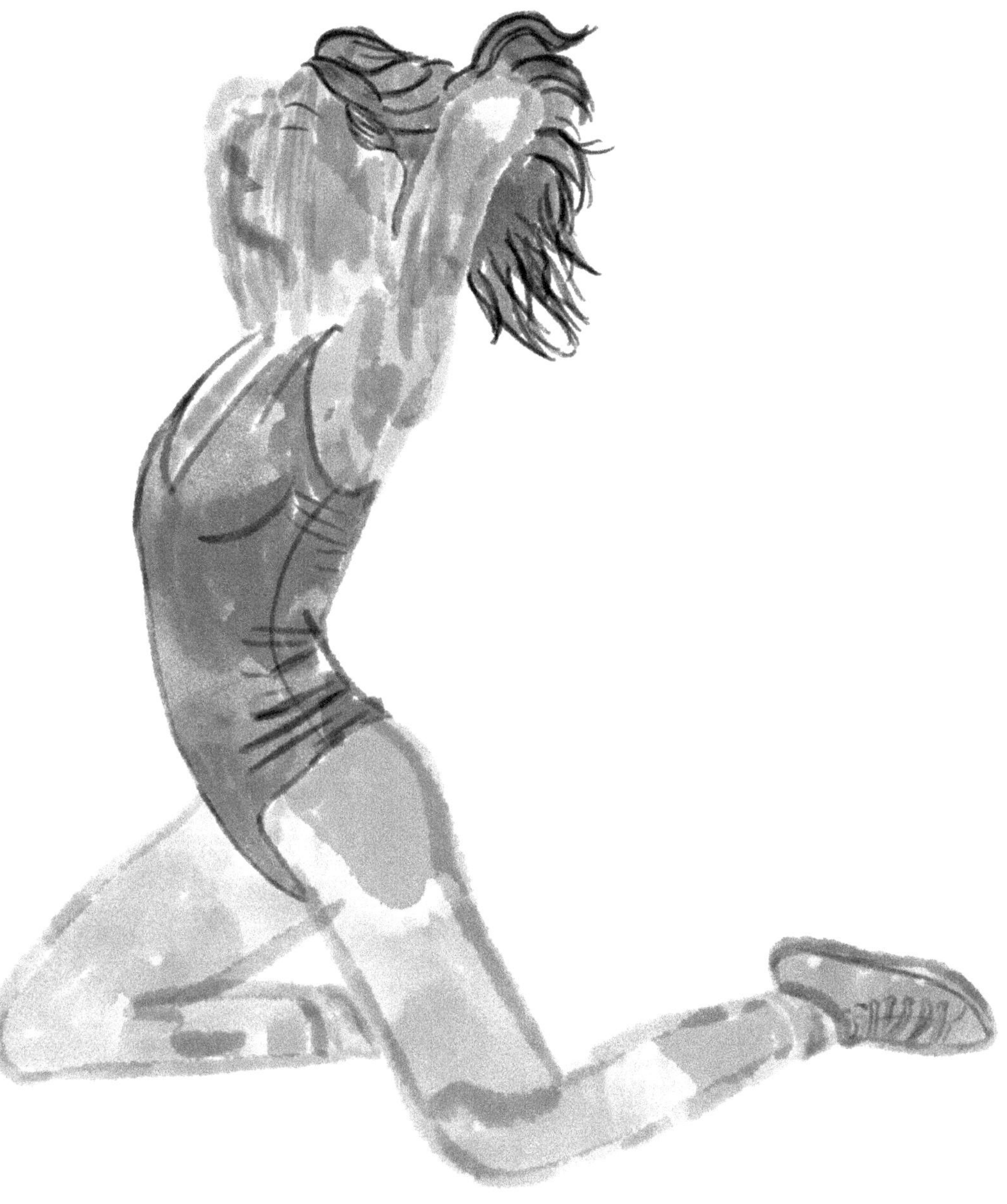

"Galaxy Girl"
2021
Digital

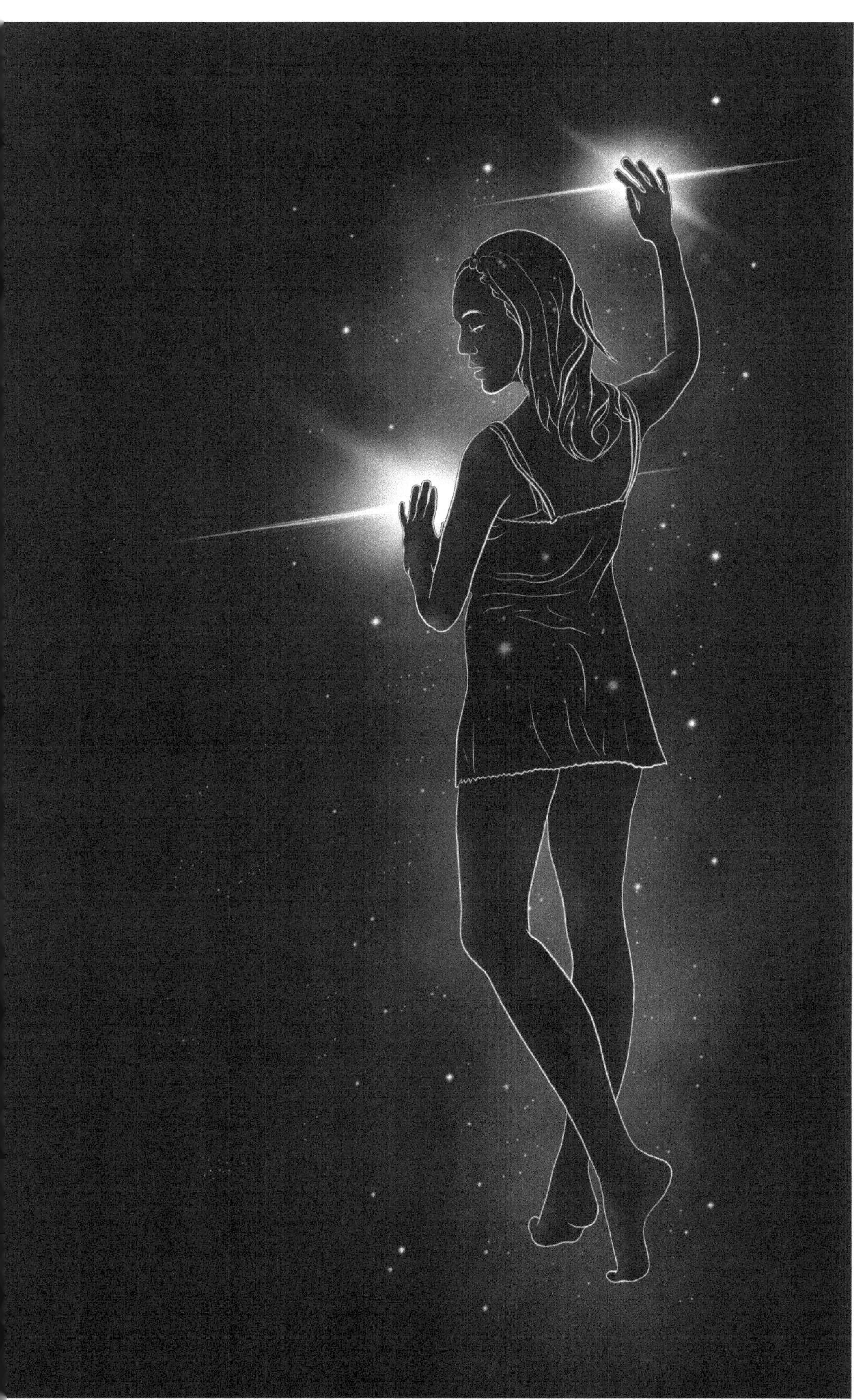

"Anatomy"
2022
Photoshop Brushes

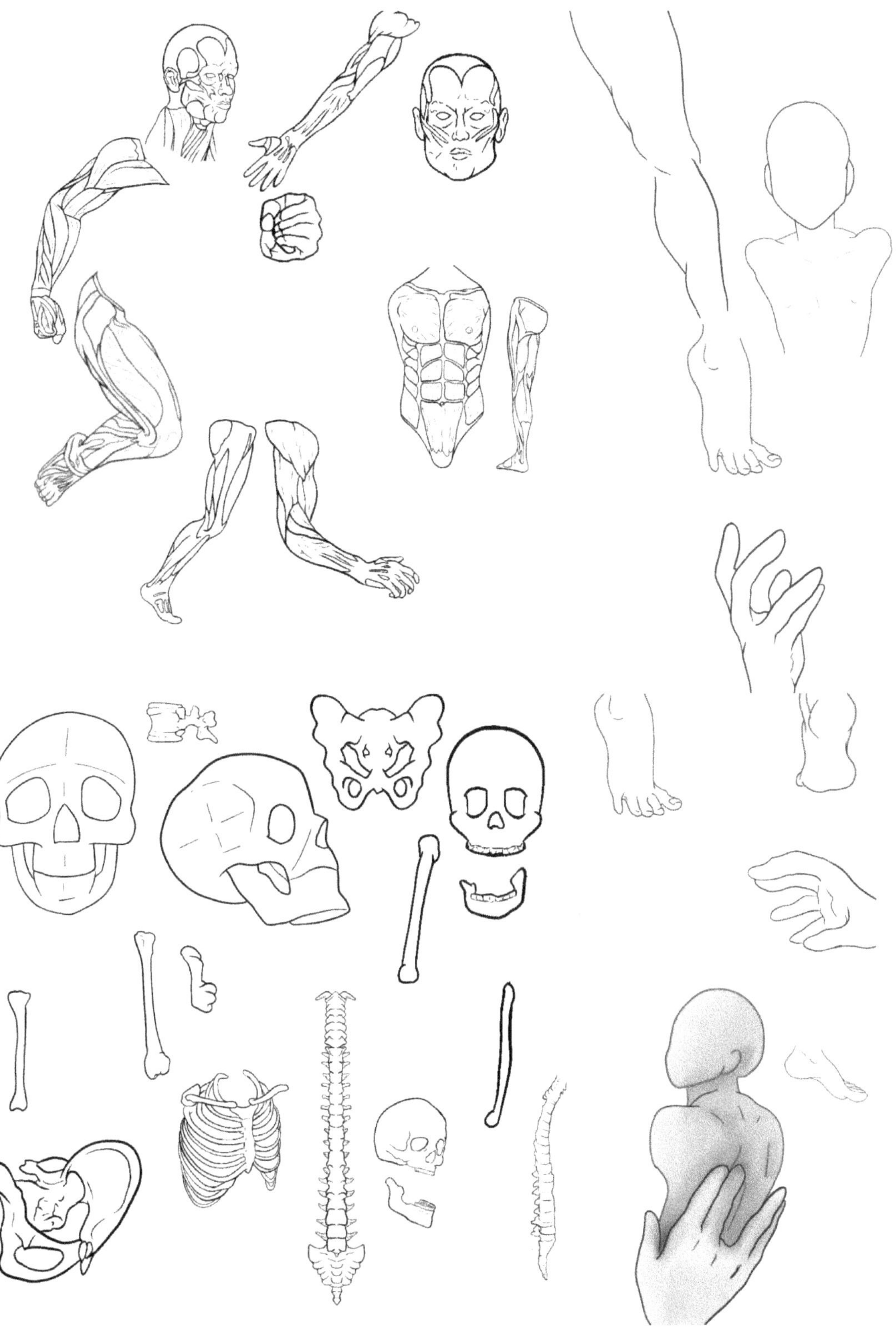

"Urban Lollipop"
2021
Photography and Photo Manipulation

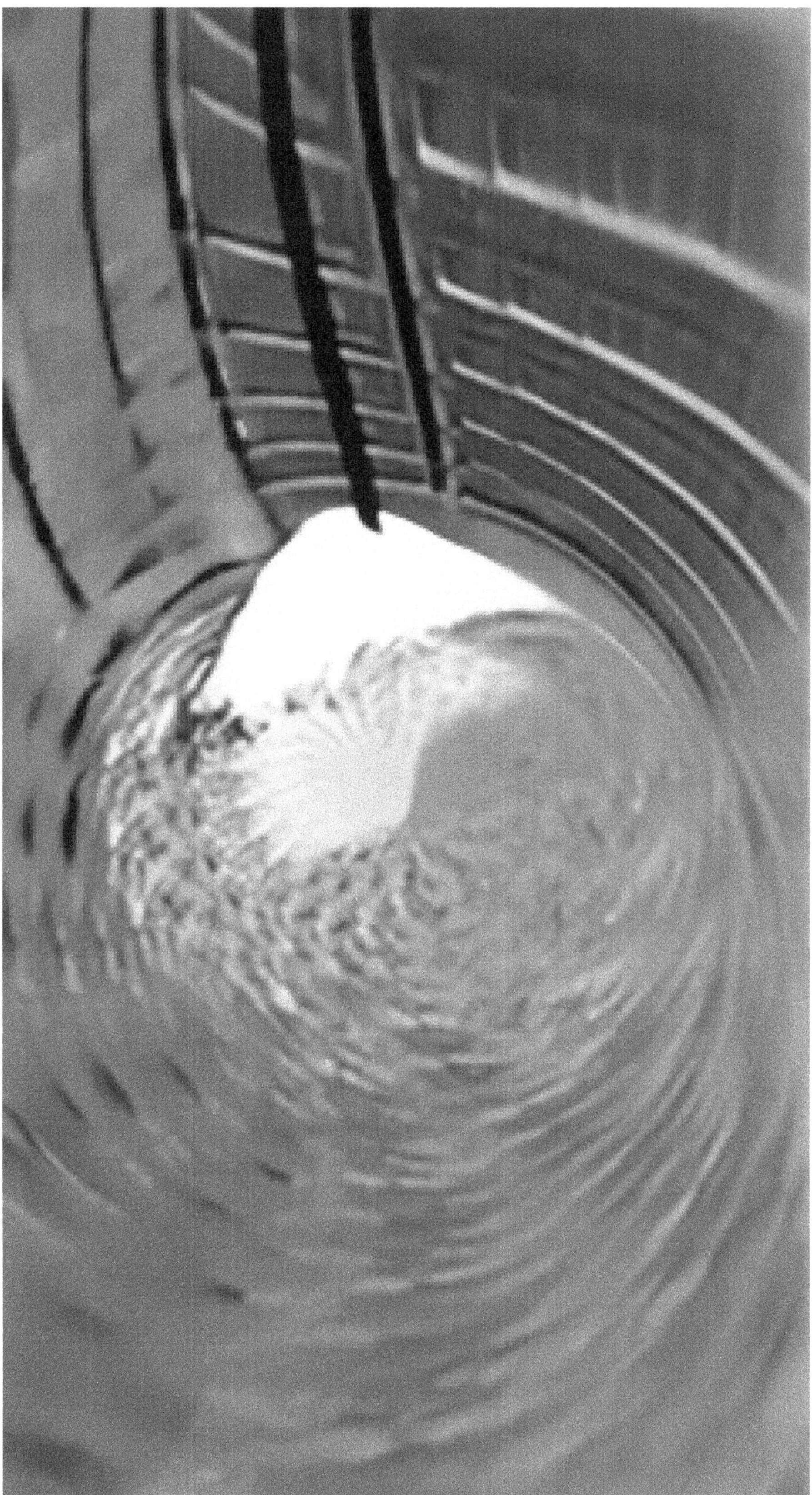

"In My Own World"
2018
360 Photography

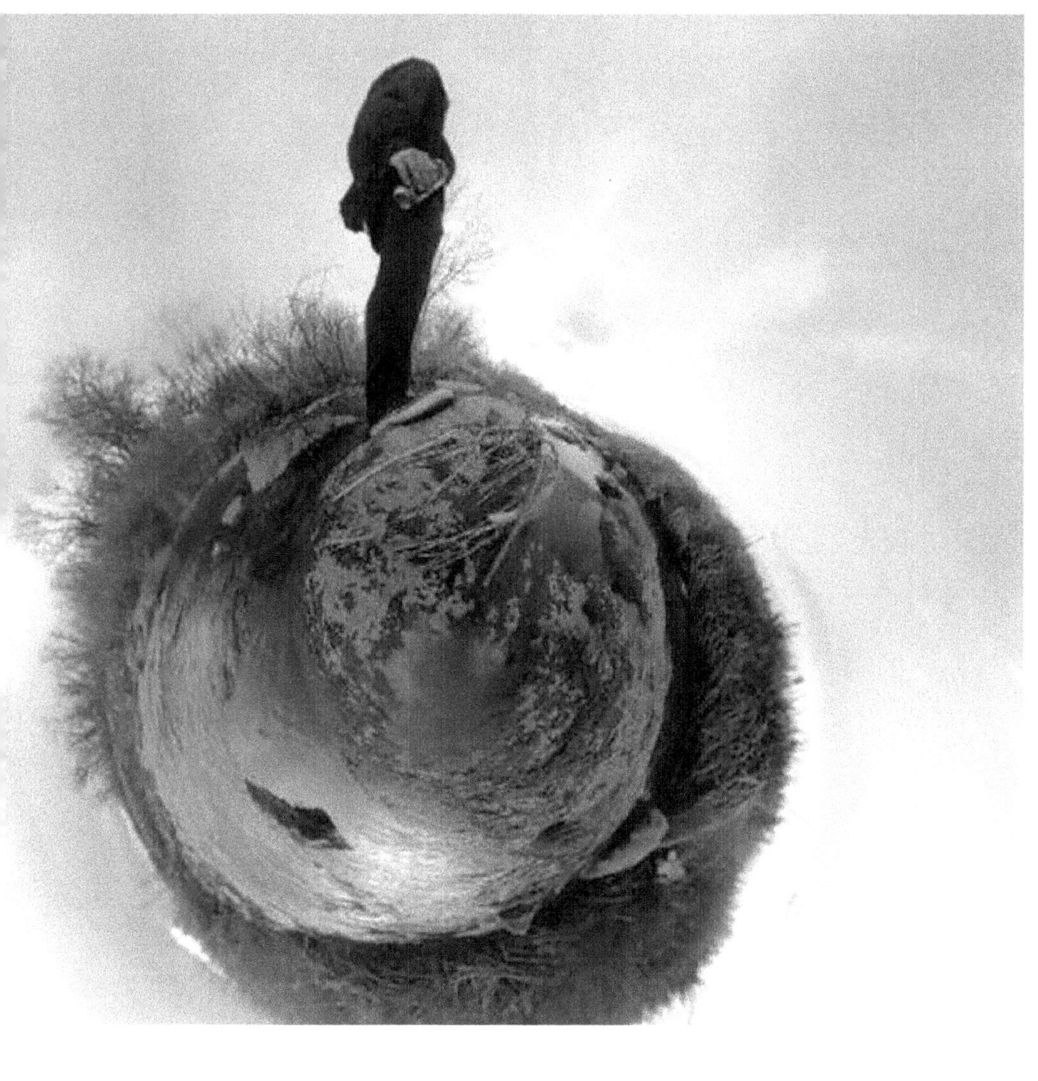

"Sisters"
2017
Graphite on Canvas

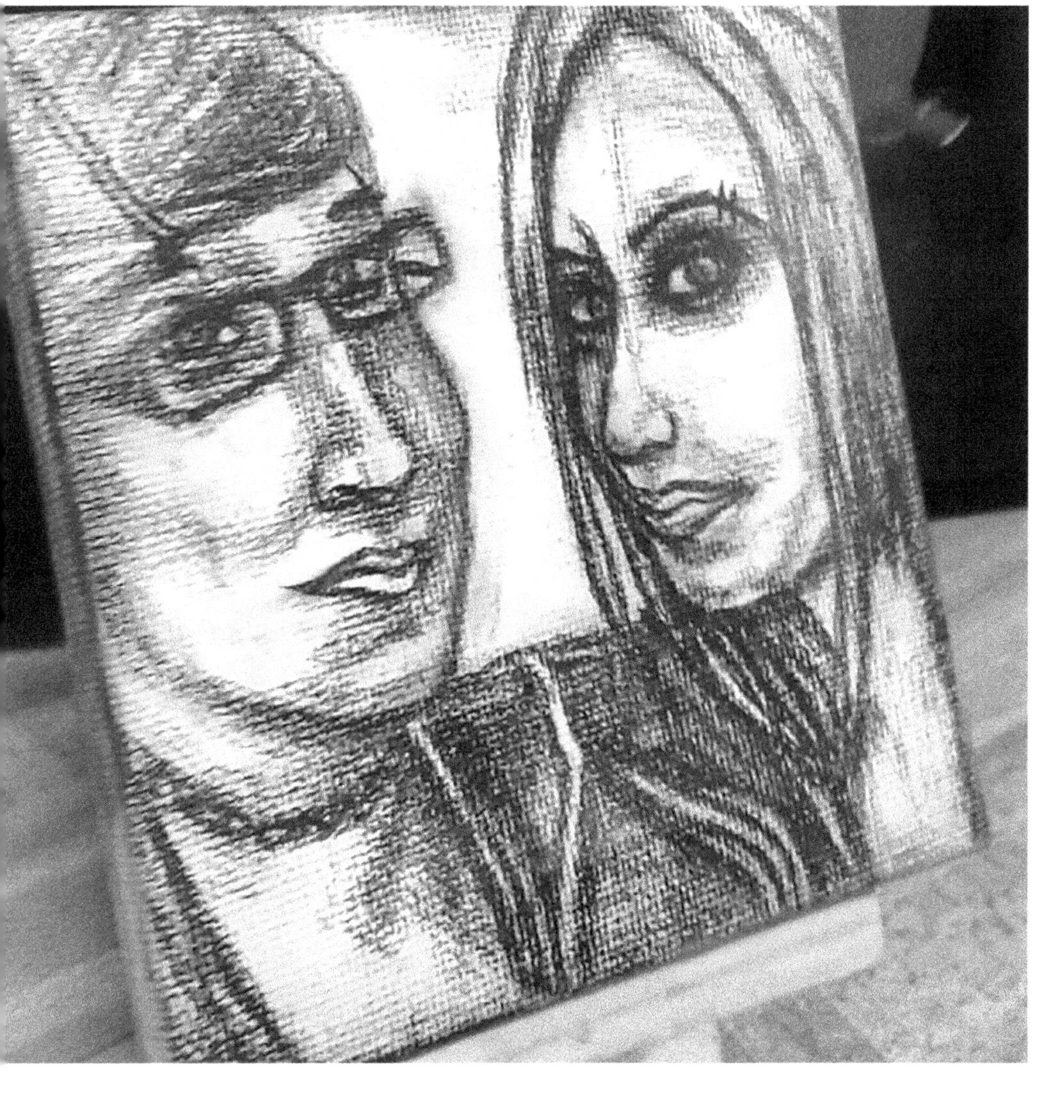

"Cheer Captain"
2020
Digital

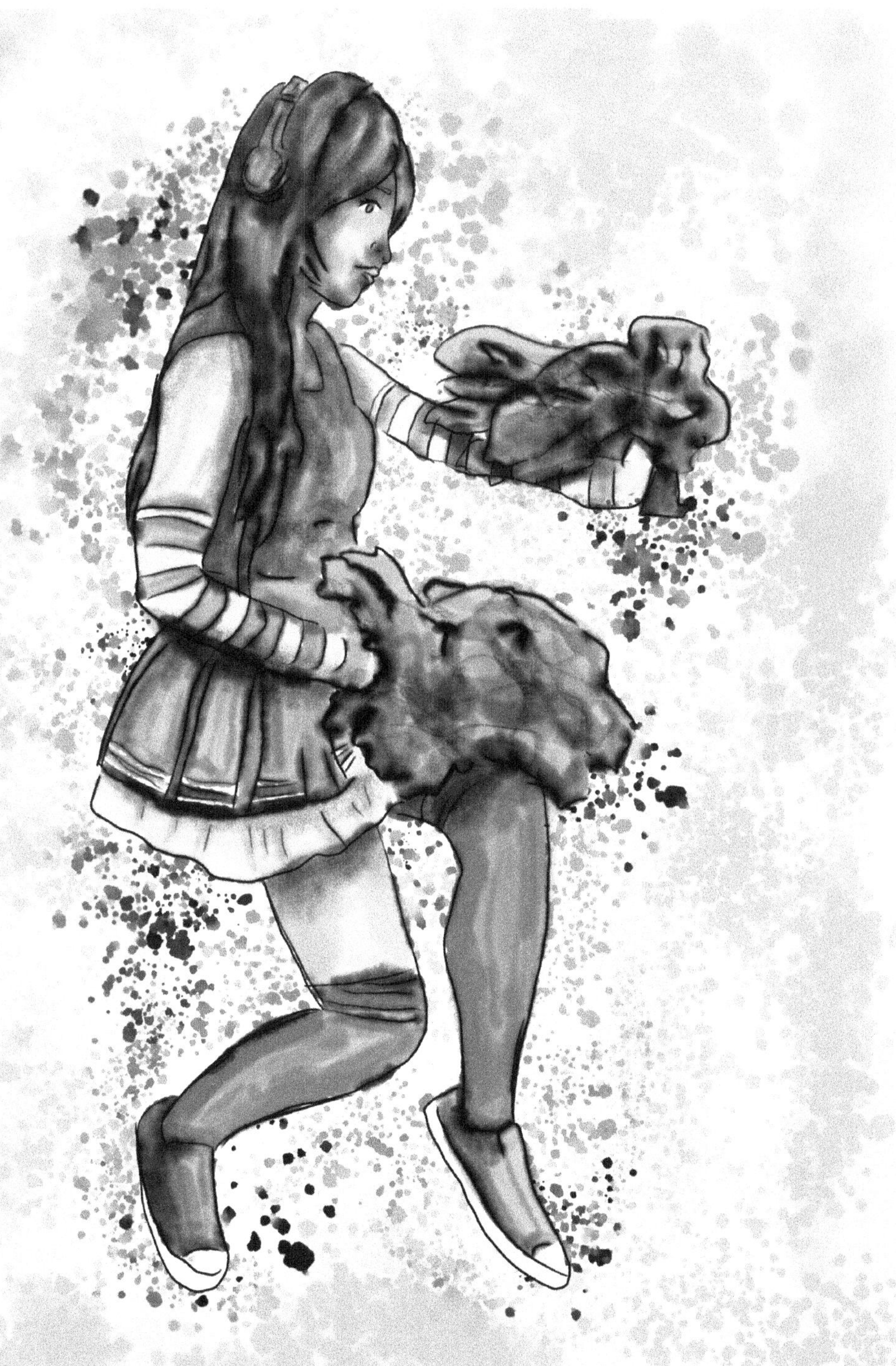

"Miami Vice"
2020
Digital

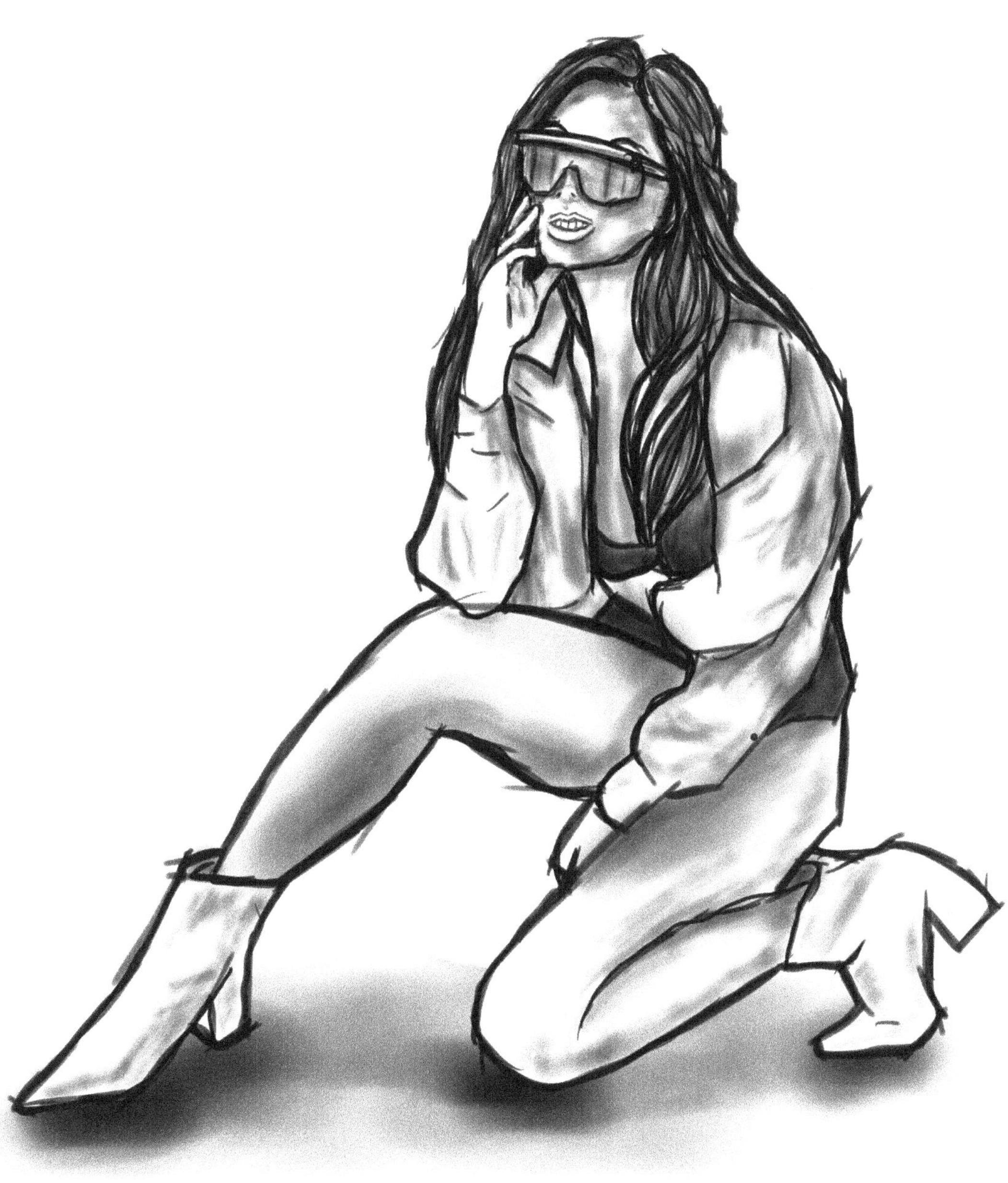

"Beach 2k16"
2016
Digital

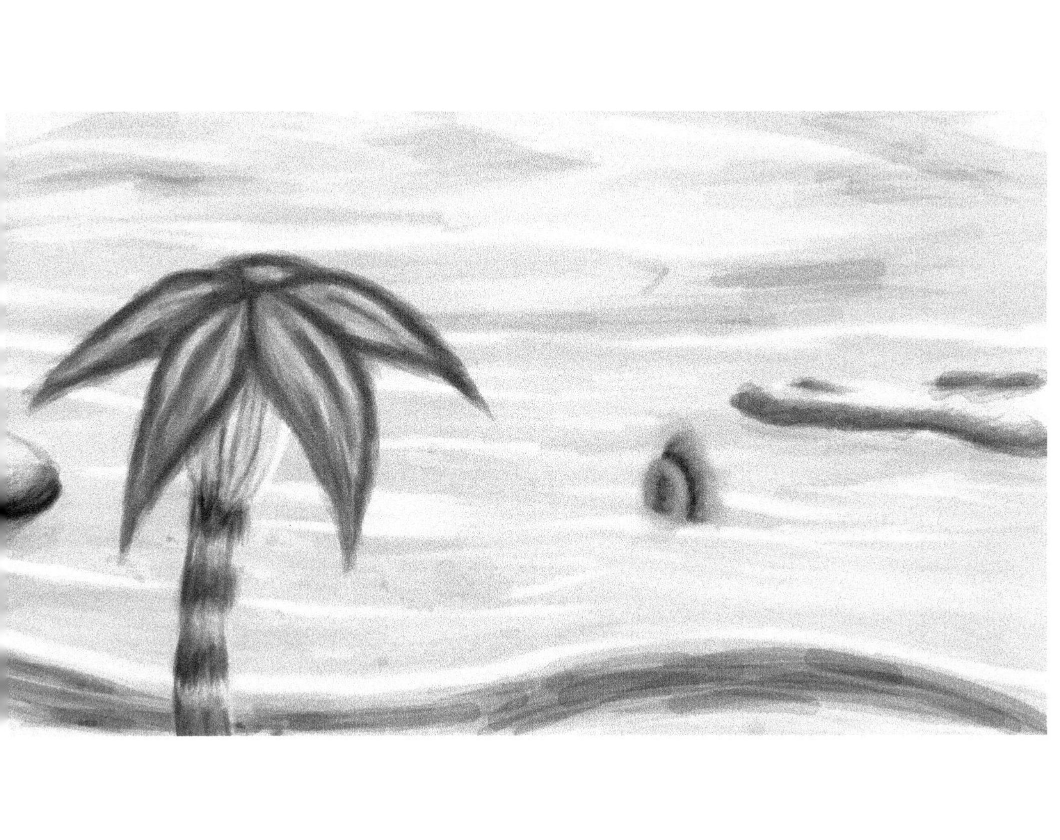

"Galactic Girl"
2019
Digital

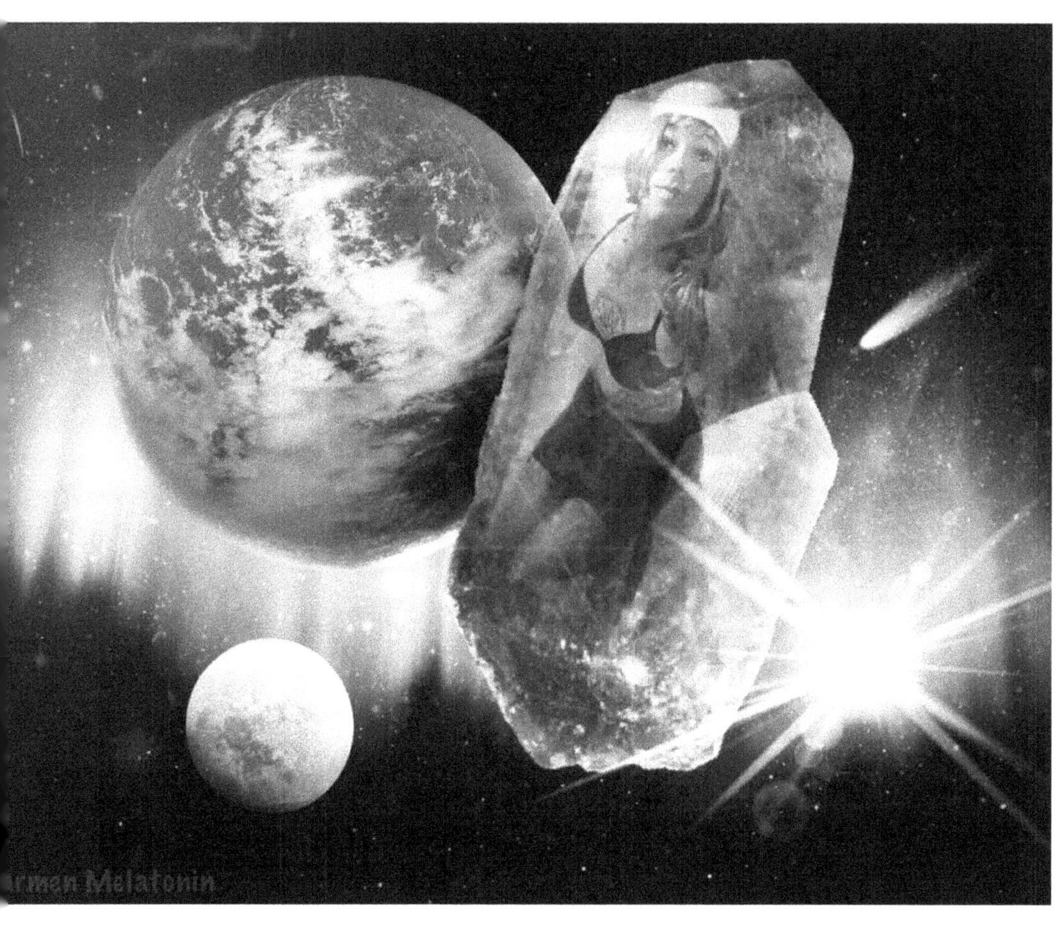
armen Melatonin

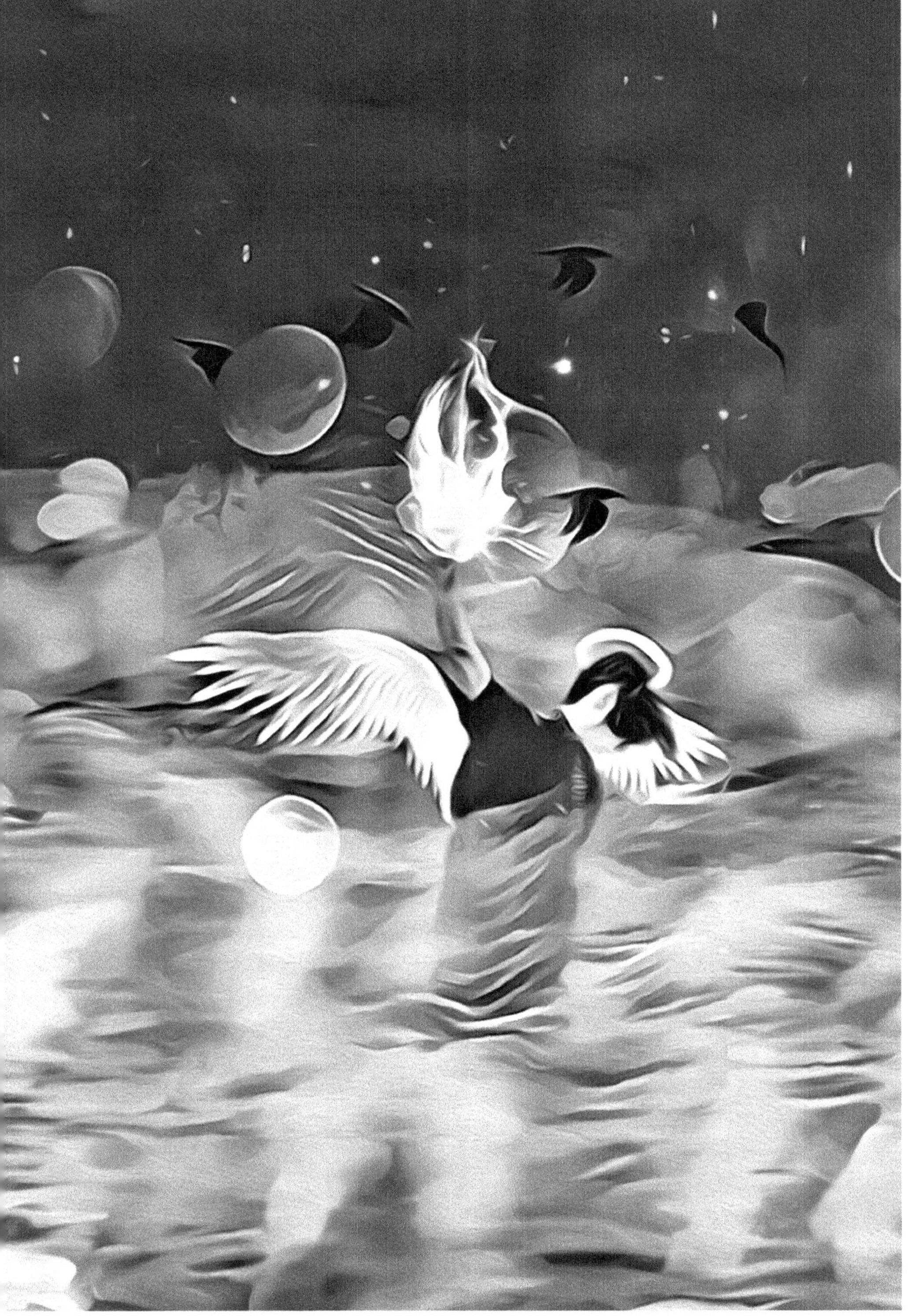

9 798330 386260